"Again, our beloved Jeshua speaks to us. His wisdom, compassion, and understanding encourage, motivate, and inspire us to remember our divine nature and to call on it daily. Not since I was introduced to "*A Course in Miracles*" have I been so deeply moved to accept that which I truly am, a child of God."
Rev. Kay Hunter, D. D.
Founding and Senior Minister
Cathedral of Light, Dallas, Texas

"Jeshua's words are so heart touching. Miracles follow miracles as you feel yourself awaken to the loving truth of who you are. It is powerful and life changing. Jeshua and Judith, thank you for blessing us all with your gifts of love."
Lynne Cox,
Relationship Counselor, Educator, Author of "Beaming Bright, You're a Shining Light."
www.ShiningLight.ca

"Thank you from the depths of my being to Jeshua and Judith who together bring us the truth of love in a way that is instantly remembered from within each heart who places their "eyes" upon this book....it is a golden treasure...to be held deep within our hearts."
Denisa, Author and channel for Jeshua.
www.thebridgetohome.com

You Are the Power of Now

*Messages from
Jeshua ben Joseph (Jesus)*

Jeshua
The Personal Christ
Volume VI

Copyright © 2011 Judith Coates

All rights reserved. Printed in the United States of America. No part of this book may be reproduced or transmitted in any form or by any means without the prior consent of the Publisher or Judith Coates, except for brief quotes used in connection with reviews written specifically for inclusion in magazines, newspapers or the internet.

ISBN 978-1-878555-16-8

**Published by
Oakbridge University Press**

Graphic design: Thomas Coates

**www.Oakbridge.org
Judith@oakbridge.org**

The messages in this book are based on transcripts of Jeshua Evenings sponsored by Oakbridge University and Press.

Heartfelt thanks to all, seen and unseen, who have assisted in the preparation of this book.

A special thanks to Maryann Moon for her continuing friendship and inspiration, and to Ted Meske for his transcribing and proofreading.

Contents

Foreword	9
The Temple of the Sun	11
The New Consciousness	19
Energy	23
Belief	31
Manifesting Your Desires	39
Unlimited Possibilities	45
Dreams and Desires	53
What Are You Waiting For?	61
The Secret of Receiving	69
Prophecies and the End of a Cycle	75
The Voice of the Brotherhood	85
The New Decade (Joseph/St. Germain)	91
The Measure of Mastery	99
Let Not Your Heart Be Troubled	105
The Origin and Future of Planet Earth	111

Cross-Culture Multiculturalism	119
Your Lineage	127
Positive Ions	133
Fifth Dimensional Perspective	141
Starseeds of the Future	149
Visionaries	157
The Ascension of the Collective Consciousness	163
The Necessity for Love (Joseph/St. Germain)	169
Memories	177
You Are the Power of Now	185
The Hologram of Now	191

Parables

The Parable of the Camel Trader	199
The Parable of the Widow	205
The Parable of the Princess in the Castle	209

Foreword

"Beloved and holy and only Child of our heavenly Father, Child of the one Source, Child of Light divine: That is who you are: Child of Light, divine." This is the way Jeshua addresses everyone at every session. He sees the non-separation of our Oneness. He sees only One.

He always tells us to contemplate what that means. Within His infinite Love, Oneness is the cornerstone of His consciousness. He always points out that we are no different than He is. On page 46 He says "...I walk *with* you. I walk *within* you as the divine expression of holy energy, Intelligence...." Thus, He has re-emphasized His immortal words, "Lo, I am with you always." He once told a group a number of years ago, "I Am Universal Mind."

We are very fortunate to have a Master Mind to help us attain a New Age consciousness. In this volume of *Jeshua, The Personal Christ* are to be found extraordinarily simple, but exceptionally profound words of wisdom that lift our minds to a much higher perspective of consciously seeing how our future is going to unfold as we go through the turbulent changing of the Ages that we are now witnessing. As always when we are reading new ideas that expand an awareness of our divinity, it is best to contemplate those new ideas, to peer deeply into them, to meditate upon those ideas and to keep those ideas at the forefront of our attention until we understand clearly. Knocking on the door of our heart always opens that door to let us know more of Who we really are.

To be a clear channel for Jeshua's words takes a strong 24/7 commitment, day in and day out dedication to this work, which pretty much eliminates having a personal life. This Judith Coates has done for nearly 20 years. If it were not for her complete dedication, the Master's words would not be available to us. When we look elsewhere in this world, these six volumes of His words are rare. Thank you, Judith, for all your tireless efforts.

This volume is rich in the spiritual clarity that is so characteristic of Jeshua's gentle, loving manner. The best part is that He is always available to anyone who knocks on the door of the Heart. It is good to remember His words, "I walk *with* you and *within* you."

Don Knight, Unity minister (retired)

Author: "Perfection - Living the New Age Life"

The Temple of the Sun

Beloved one, once upon a time, before there was time, there was and is and forever will be outside of time an Isness, a consciousness, if you will, an Intelligence that will be forever beyond time. It exists now, as you understand time, and it will exist forever, as you understand time, because time is limited. You feel that in your daily lives. You feel the limitations of time.

"I have to be somewhere at a certain time," and you rush about. Sometimes you chafe, because certain schedules keep you waiting. I know that your time is precious. I thank you for sharing your time in this way with me.

But once upon a time, before there was time, you were and are and always will be the Intelligence of the One. As the free-flowing Intelligence of the Creator, the creative One, there was a Thought to create. From that one moment outside of time, you as an aspect of the One created all realities: realities within time and realities outside of time.

Now, there are many more realities outside of time than within time. That is a bit difficult to understand as you struggle each day with your daily activities. But it is also something that you know very deep within you as you chafe against the schedules.

You know that there is instantaneous manifestation. You know that it does not have to take time in order to heal. You know this from other lifetimes, whether it be in realities that believed and were based on time or realities outside of time. You know it deeply within yourself that you are an expansive being, and that is why you chafe against the small ego when it comes up with limitations and says, "But you are only one person, and you have a limited time span for this lifetime. That which you want to become or make manifest, you probably won't."

Separated ego often says that. It says that because you have asked it to say that scripting so that you can prove it wrong, and it does your bidding. It runs right onstage and it says, "Ah, you'll never be able to be wealthy, prosperous. You'll never be able to manifest a loving mate or a friend who will love you no matter what. You will never be able to know that the loved ones who have released the body and have gone on are still with you. You'll never know that."

That is what separated ego says to you. But then the loved one who has gone on speaks to you, and you say, "Well, they can't be speaking to me. They are no longer here."

They are here. And separated ego runs back onstage and says, "How do you know? Can you prove it?" And you say, "Well, there's a feeling. I feel the loved one with me, and if I feel it, there has to be something. I'm not quite sure what, and I can't define it, and there probably aren't words for it, but I feel it."

And separated ego says, "Oh, okay," and goes off in the wings, offstage for awhile until the next time it is called forth.

When we first thought to create a physical reality, we created light, the vibration of light, and with that the vibration of sound, as you understand the physical laws. We created most harmonious manifestations of Oneness.

You still have that. It still exists. If you ever want proof, look at your rainbow. There you have physical manifestation of different vibrations of color from one range to another through the various vibrations seen as color, and if you could hear the rainbow—and some ones can—you would hear a melody, a harmony.

When we first thought to have physical experience, we brought forth the different constellations, and they were as yet amorphous. They were as yet unformed, not as you know them now to be, and we danced as the light upon and within the amorphous constellations.

Then there was a thought to evolve into something different, because you are always—I see you doing this in your daily life—thinking of what is the next goal, what is the next project you are going to work on. We are always thinking to create more.

There became more density. The Light played with the density, and we brought forth many, many constellations in form. You now have the most wonderful pictures of light of other constellations that come to you from many, many light years away, more than what you would count a lifetime or several lifetimes to be, light now coming to you from constellations where you played at one time and then sent yourself here to receive that light in this lifetime.

So when you look in your heavens and you see the light of the various stars, know that truly you have played within those constellations, and the light that you brought forth then is coming to you now for the purpose of reminding you of how creative you are, how Light you are, how you can and do manifest.

You have chosen now to be within this reality on this third rock from the sun—as your television program has called it—and to live out lifetimes on this rock, which truly is not rock at all; it is vibration of differing densities.

When we came to play upon this firmament, we danced as the Light that we are, and we knew ourselves to be very fluid. We even went within the Earth, our holy Mother, the planet, because this reality that you call firm is not firm at all. It is changing all of the time; it is very fluid and very porous.

There are ones who remember themselves to be lighter vibration and more fluid who do live within holy Mother Earth. Sometimes you will—again, as we spoke of the loved ones—you will know a presence of them. There are certain sacred spots that ones have pointed out where you can go and be in communion with the ones who live within this planet. Have you lived within the planet? Yes, a long, long time ago as you measure time, before you decided that you wanted to live on the surface with a more solidified and defined form. But even the defined form you change from time to time. (Smile)

You have often looked to the heavens in your nighttime and have taken inspiration from the stars, or in the daytime you have looked to the sun that is so important for warmth and for the growing of the food that sustains you. For many, many lifetimes you were and still are sun worshippers. I see you as you go out in the sun and enjoy being out-of-doors in the sun.

Allow yourself to go within and to worship the sun within yourself. You are indeed a temple, a living temple of divine radiance. Live in the space of light, forgetting all else that is happening around you for a moment or so—or if it be possible, for longer than that—and allow the temple of the sun within to be your focus.

Feel the power of the physical sun. You know the power of the physical sun. You know how warm it can be. You know how powerful it is every day as it arises. And you know the lifetimes when you have worshipped it for its life-giving properties.

But the sun in your heavens is no comparison to the sun within you, that divine essence within you, out of which you create everything.

You are the temple of the Sun of yourself. So if you have been worrying about something, allow yourself to take a deep breath...right now...feel that easy, deep breath and allow yourself to go within, eyes open or eyes closed, whichever feels comfortable, and go within to the sacred place of the Sun within you, and know that within you is divine radiance.

There is nothing that can threaten or change the divine radiance within you. Feel it with your mind's eye. Feel yourself in the Sun within yourself. Know that you are surrounded by the Sunlight that you are. Feel it. Visualize it. Allow it to expand until you feel yourself to be in a bubble of Sunlight. Feel yourself to be safe, secure within the Sunlight of yourself.

All that you have ever truly desired abides within the Sun within your own temple, within yourself. Go within and for a moment allow everything else to be blotted out by the brilliance of the Sun in that space. Visualize how the Sun fills every part of your being. Visualize yourself in the middle of that Sun. Feel its warmth. Feel its power. Feel the security. Nothing can threaten that security.

Any time that the world speaks to you of problems, go quickly to your own temple and to your Sun and abide there in the security of the divine essence, the divine radiance that you are.

And then if there is something that has been troubling you, bring it within that light and see how it dissolves into nothing, into light, knowing yourself always to be taken care of, always in the Light.

You have fashioned a body so that you could walk through this reality to play in this reality, to struggle with all of the challenges that you have collectively agreed upon. But none of those challenges can threaten or change the divine Light of you within you.

All you have to do is take that one breath and go within to the candlelight within — if sometimes you feel that your Sun is not quite as big as you would like it to be.

You can visualize the candle flame and then see it expanding to fill all of the mind's eye. And wait, because sometimes there will be inspiration. Sometimes there will be guidance, an idea that comes out of the Light that has been there all of the time within the Light, but you have not yet given it opportunity to come forth.

Sometimes all you need is to know the security of that Light, to know that you are loved in that Light, and that always you will be loved and taken care of.

You are the temple of the Sun. Even as you are walking through the darkness of the valley of the world, you are the Light of this world. That is what you said you would do in this lifetime by various journeys, by various means, various occupations.

Never do you need to worry about anything. Hear me well when I say that. I am the demonstration of that, as you are the demonstration of it. My lifetime was fraught with challenges, threats, even crucifixion. Look at my lifetime and take courage from that lifetime. You will not be asked to give over the body, and even if you were, that is not who you are. The body is not who you are. But you will not be asked to give over the body until you choose to give it over.

My story is your story. In other lifetimes you have known physical crucifixion. In many other lifetimes you have known emotional crucifixion; even in this lifetime you crucify yourself daily emotionally by listening to the words of separated ego. But you do not have to. You can come down off of the cross and live in the Light: you can find the temple of the Sun within yourself.

So any time when the outward appearances of things look to be threatening or suggest loss or abandonment or rejection, go quickly to the temple of the Sun within yourself. In your mind's eye, even if you are standing in a crowd of people with your eyes open, you can still in the mind's eye see yourself in that Sun and know that always— this is my guarantee unto you; I have been there, I have done it, I have tried it, I have tested it, and I know it to be true— you will always be taken care of in the temple of your own Sun within.

That is what it means when we speak of the Christ of you. It is your own Sun within you, the brilliance, the divine radiance of the Christ of you. So whenever the world speaks to you, go within to that place of the Sun within yourself. Make your choice from the place of the Sun.

The Christ of you abides in the Sun, in the divine brilliance and radiance within you, and that will always bring you Home. I know this to be true, so I speak it to you.

So be it.

The New Consciousness

You have brought forth a new consciousness. It is a consciousness which truly has been in process for some time, both for you individually and for the collective. You have been, again, the one who has been on the cutting edge, on the crest of the wave. The master that you are, you have come one more time to participate in an evolutionary step in the realization of Oneness.

We have spoken in previous times of how this reality is based upon an experiment, if you will, of starseeds, each and every one of you having come from different star constellations and having been the descendants of ones from other star constellations, bringing with you remembrance of life and cultures in other places and other realities.

The evolution that you have agreed that you will take part in is being watched by many of the brothers and sisters who are not incarnate in human form. They may be incarnate in other forms or not incarnate at all.

In this experiment you agreed that you would see if it could be and how it could be achieved to bring ones to a place of understanding the divinity of each point of Light, and to come to a place of respect to truly treasure the diversity of the cultures which have come from the various star constellations.

It has been very much an evolutionary process, and you are now at a most wonderful place. You have been waking up in this lifetime from a deep slumber. You agreed, as the masters which you are, that you would take upon yourself the raiment of the human embodiment and you would take upon yourself the role of forgetting.

Now you are seeing the achievement of what has been in process for a long time, where many of the brothers and sisters have awakened to their power; not worldly power, truly, although they may understand it as worldly power, but the power of themselves and what they believe in.

Those who have had power in the past and have used it in their own arena have done what they needed to do to bring you to a certain point in this process. So I say unto you to honor the ones who have gone before, because they have brought the collective consciousness to a place of clarity in choosing. The ones who came before had a role to play and played it well.

I have spoken to you over the years how everything serves the atonement, and there were times when you did not believe me. You said, "Yes, but look what is happening all around me. This cannot be serving the atonement, the holy atonement. Look how ones are treating others. How can this serve the atonement?"

Well, it has brought you and the collective consciousness to a most wonderful place where brothers and sisters who have felt themselves to be without power, to be powerless, have found that they had a voice and that they could envision a better way to live with their neighbors.

The belief in a reality built upon separation is now being re-examined and looked at differently, for it has been thought for many eons of time that the powerful ones would collect unto themselves their supporters and they would be the only powerful ones.

As you have watched much of the division which has happened, you have doubted and you have cried unto me and to my mother, Mary, and you have said, "Please release me from this world. I don't want to be in this kind of reality."

Now you have seen that the reality itself can be changed, that you do not have to be taken out of it. For truly, you have agreed that you will be in it in order to make the changes.

The new consciousness is here. Now, the new consciousness is a bit like the newborn. It is going to need some nurturing. It is going to need some support. It is going to need voices that say, "Look what happens when we believe that there can be change. Look what happens when we exercise hope and have a new vision."

There are going to be ones who are going to doubt that this new energy can last, so you are going to treat this new consciousness with some nurturing by visioning, truly knowing deep within yourself that you can bring forth change, that you do manifest your reality moment by moment by that which you believe to be possible: envision, know, trust, speak.

It is a great time to be incarnate. Many of you have wondered about that. I think each and every one of you, in your quiet times, has said to me, "Why am I here? Why did I choose this lifetime? Why…" It is because of Now. It is because of the new consciousness that you have been preparing for yourself and for the collective, a process which began a long, long time ago when you reached the level of the greatest density and asked, from your soul, "Does it have to be so dark, so dense?" With that moment of inspiration, of connecting with Original Spirit, you began the process of remembering at-One-ment. It has taken you lifetimes, many generations lived in different cultures, to come to this Now point of seeing some Light.

Keep the vision. Speak. Trust. Trust that always, when you come from the place of the heart, that which you speak will be in love. It may not always be received in love immediately, but you will be allowing love to be in that space.

Speak what you know. This lifetime you can, and you will, because you have seen through the cracks in the wall. You have seen what beckons unto you. You have seen, you and the brothers and sisters, each one as a seemingly singular drop of water in the vast ocean coming together as the ocean, and you know the power of the ocean as it rolls onto the sand

and the beach. You know the power of the ocean when it is One; not just thinking itself to be separate, just a drop of water in the ocean, but One. Now, there is power even as you see yourself to be a singular drop of water, because if a singular drop of water keeps dripping on the same stone over and over and over, it makes an indentation. It makes a mark. You, even in times when you think yourself to be a lone voice, make a mark on the collective consciousness.

There is now a new consciousness, a new belief in what the divine Self can manifest. It will be a process, but a very important evolution has occurred. Envision, hope, trust, speak. Remember how it feels to be truly alive, knowing that you have the divine power.

Energy

I would speak with you now about energy. Imagine for a moment a sphere, any size that you want to imagine. We will take one perhaps twelve inches across just as an example, but it can be as big as you want it to be. Within that sphere are many points which are connected by energy to each other so that to appearances it would be a solid, dense sphere.

But in truth, in between every point of energy there is much space, the same as your scientists now are teaching you about your universe, that there is truly more space than there are objects that have collected themselves into the denser form of energy in any dimension.

You have brought forth the sphere and all of the points within it. Not only that, but you have said that the sphere of experience is infinite, which means that what you would understand in this reality as having boundaries to make a sphere is truly open-ended with no boundaries. But your reality yet understands boundaries and says that everything has to have a beginning, a middle, and an ending. Every box has to have sides to it. But I am speaking to you now of infinite energy.

You interact with every point within the infinite sphere and, because the distance from one point to another point is perceived as a line, you see it as a linear timeline and you say, "Past lives, future lives, present life, present connections, etc.," but in truth, it is all happening at the same time, which is a non-time.

Now, in this reality that truth boggles the mind a bit, because this reality, for security reasons, wants to know, "How far towards the edge can I go before I fall off? I want a boundary somewhere so that I can know myself to be safe within that boundary."

But in truth, you are always safe, you are always expanding, and when the purpose of time, as you have built it into this reality, has been fulfilled — in other words, the moment that you realize that you are not bounded by time at all — time will no longer exist.

You have agreed before an incarnation that, as the energy you are, you will interact with other points of energy in what is called the soul group and with others in what appear to be other soul groups. The ones who are in resonance with each other, regarding vibratory level, often agree that they will come and find each other no matter where or in what geographical country or location they may be. You find a nudging that pushes you to somewhere and you meet up with friends of the soul group who have agreed that they will be incarnate at the same time as you.

You have done this over and over many times so that you could play together, so that you could support each other, so that you could move forward in the enlightenment of the collective. So once again you have agreed that no matter where the physical body may be residing, you will know yourself to be infinite energy connecting with all others who are also awakening to what they have felt deep within their heart: knowing that the human life is good, but it is not all there is; knowing each day to look for the positive, the good, the blessing in each day.

That is not the message of the world, but it is the message of Truth. For as a particle of energy, you cannot help but attract, as a magnet does, other energy to you, and it takes different forms. You have built that into your reality because you wanted to play with different appearances, different experiences, and then to judge them. And often they get judged in a negative way.

Begin by counting your blessings. Look around right now and see all of the blessings you have gathered to your experience. Look on the positive side of everything. If you do not see the positive side of something right away, flip it. Say, "Okay, here is this experience. This is how it looks to me now. Now I'm going to walk around it and see something different." Look at it from all angles. If it is not apparent right away, search until you find the blessing in it; it will not be hidden from you.

You have magnetized it. You have brought it to you. You are the creator of everything you experience; therefore, you are the master of it. So there is nothing, no thing, no condition, no experience that is more powerful than you. You are the master of it.

Throughout lifetimes, because of the sadness of feeling far from Home and outside of Love, you have reinforced for yourself over and over the feeling of unworthiness. The truth of the matter is, you are very strong. Only the strongest ones, only the masters call to themselves that which would be seen to be difficult and challenging. Let that sink in for a moment. Only the masters would have the courage to say, "Okay, let me try that experience. I want to know that experience from the inside out; not just to look at it as an appearance that maybe somebody else is experiencing, but I want to know it from the inside."

And so then your wish is granted, and you get to experience various challenges, as the world would call them, but actually they are blessings. You get to experience them intimately to the place where you begin to understand that you *are* the point of energy. You *are* in the infinite sphere of energy that is forever ongoing, forever creating, and will, past any limitation of time, exist and create and create. Let that sink in.

When you begin to realize how powerful you are, there is a freedom that comes, a freedom that the world does not know, a freedom that says, "I do not have to worry what this day is going to bring me, because I know it is going to be all good. I know that the world may present it in a certain way, but what does the world know?"

The world only knows a set of paradigms that has been lived over and over and over and has truly been completed. Understand this: the world only knows that which has already been completed. So when you wake up — and I mean literally in the morning when you wake up — and you say, "This day is a gift. This day is mine. I have made this day for myself," then there is the freedom to live in a new paradigm of joy, of security in knowing that you have never truly left Home. You have extended yourself as a rubber band, perhaps, into a reality that believes that there could be other than Love, but you are the rubber band that is its point of origin and at any moment can snap right back to the place of Love, the place of Home.

Allow yourself to see the body as energy, because truly that is what it is. It feels like there are limitations to it, but in truth, you are energy that is forever mixing around in the body all of the time. Even as you think you are just sitting on a chair or lying on the bed, that energy in you is always moving around, coming to different formations. Some of the formations you keep for awhile. Others of the formations just move on and go into another formation.

You do a miracle in bringing the body into the form that you consciously know as your body. It is a miracle that you carry from moment to moment to moment, and when you wake up in the morning, again you assume the same focus of what the body is going to be. A moment before you woke up, what was that body doing? In truth, it was moving around, as the energy that it is, being amorphous, without shape.

Now, someone who walks into the room is going to see shape. Why? Expectancy; what they have known from lifetime to lifetime to lifetime in this reality to be true. But in Truth, you are energy that is moving all of the time. Every part of the body is moving. As I speak with you right now, there are synapses in the brain that are firing, going off, allowing the message to be taken in in a certain way.

Every muscle, every organ in the body is moving as the energy that it is, forming, reforming. You know this from your science which studies anatomy and the functioning of the body. The stomach and intestines are very busy all of the time. They are squeezing and squeezing, letting up, squeezing, relief. The heart is pumping the blood. It is squeezing, releasing, squeezing, resting, squeezing, etc.

Truly, you are a walking ball of energy that you have fashioned into a form that you understand to be you and that others understand to be you, yet it is always in motion and always changing. Sometimes the most wonderful thing happens to prove this to you. If you have not seen a friend in some years and you meet up with them say ten or twenty years later, their form has changed. Now, how did that happen? If they are one form and they are rigid form, they would always be that form. But you meet up with them later and they look different. Sometimes you do not even recognize them. And then they start to speak and you say, "Oh, yes, it's you. Oh, okay."

I want you to understand how malleable, how changeable the body is. It responds to your thoughts. Now, you have heard that your thoughts create your reality. In truth, that is really what happens. If you go around feeling that it is really, really a struggle to be here and you wonder, "I don't know why everybody has left me"...If you are going to be a sad sack, people *are* going to leave you. They do not want to be around that energy any more than you want to be around that energy. But if you get up in the morning and you are really ready for this day, feeling, "I want to see what this day is going to bring. I am so happy, I wake up laughing" — and you can literally wake up laughing — your day is going to be fun.

Wake yourself up tomorrow morning laughing at a dream that you may or may not remember, but wake up laughing. It can be done. And say to yourself, "This day is going to be full of laughter. It's going to be full of blessings. It is going to mirror back to me the affirmation of my self-worth as to how worthy I am to be the divine holy innocent Child living the human experience."

No longer do you need to feel stuck in what the world has said reality has to be. That is where freedom comes in. When you realize that the world has not made you, you have made the world, then it has no power over you. *You* are the maker of you. And if you are the maker of you and you do not like what you are experiencing, change the script.

Allow yourself to feel free. If there are things that you want to change in your life and they seem really big, start with one step and another step and then another step, but start. Do not just sit and say, "Oh, it's a mountain; I'll never be able to climb up over that." Well, of course, you cannot if that is your attitude. But if you begin by saying, "Well, I can climb a little way up that mountain…" then you get up a way and you look back and you say, "Oh, I see a valley. I must have come a way up the mountain." And then you go a little farther and a little farther.

Every so-called challenge is seen in a new way as you will *start* with a willingness. The only thing you have to have is a willingness to see things differently; to begin to visualize yourself as the ball of energy that is forever moving and changing; changing shape within yourself, and in the outer, as well.

Many of you, if you get tired of a certain appearance, you cut your hair; it makes a change. Sometimes you change the color of your hair. Sometimes you will change the raiment so that you look a bit different. Sometimes you decide to go on what is called the diet and you lose a bit of weight, and so you change the form.

All of the time you are moving energy. You are not solid. There is nothing solid about the body, nothing that cannot be changed. That is one of the beautiful freedoms which comes with the awareness that, that which is at this moment in a certain shape and condition can be changed in whatever way you want to change it.

So if you had several people lined up with the same body condition, and person "A" chooses to eat only raw food and they know that that is going to be their healer, the way they are going to heal, okay; person "B" says he is going to go with a certain pharmaceutical substance which has, in Truth, been devised by himself, because otherwise it would not exist in his consciousness; he has created it. Person "A" cannot judge person "B", and person "B" cannot judge person "A". Everyone makes their free choice as to what is their path.

As you become the beholder and you can step back and review, re-look at previous lifetimes, you will see that perhaps in this lifetime you are choosing to go the route of the pharmaceuticals. Other lifetimes you have been the raw food advocate, or vice versa. You have been on all sides of the belief systems.

Then you begin to understand just how fluid everything is—not just the body, but relationships and conditions. Even as you feel that the chair is solid and the house seems to be solid, the house is energy, and the walls are moving. Luckily, you are moving in sync with the house, with the chair, so that you do not fall through.

Everything is energy, everything is in motion, everything is fluid, everything is changeable and is changing. Nothing is ever set, except Love. Allow yourself to live in joy. Allow yourself to wake up in the morning laughing; laughing at how silly you have been the day before to have worried about whatever it was that you were worried about, and just say, "Ah, you know, I see that differently now. You know, I really tied myself up in knots yesterday about that."

And you begin to laugh. You see things differently, and the freedom that comes with seeing things differently brings you back Home. There has been a change in the energy of an old paradigm, and you have broken out of it.

Visualize the infinite sphere of energy, the points of light, the points of energy — even more than just light —

and how they are connected, how they are always working together. Visualize the body as energy, always changing, moving, very fluid, and know that the world is not your maker. *You* are in charge. You are the divine Energy which creates everything formed and unformed.

Belief

Every experience and every expression which you create comes from a vantage point, a belief as to who and what you are. You have in the consciousness and subconscious the generational beliefs which have been handed down to you from the parents, from the generations of the grandfather, great-grandfather, great-grandmother, etc. and from the peers and their generational belief embodied in the culture in which you have been raised.

Your belief is based upon what is given to you — subliminally many, many times — by the generations, by the parents, and by the peers as to what the common belief is about what life has to be. If your family is one that believes life has to be a struggle, that everything that comes to you has to be a challenge, then from the time you are very small — even before that, in truth; as you are in the mother's womb — there is a receptivity of energy, a receptivity which may interpret that life is hard, it is a struggle.

Or, the perception can be that life is joyful, and if the mother is looking forward to having this new one born and there is a great anticipation and welcoming of the new one, the new one is going to know and will feel that joy, even in the womb before it is out in the arms.

After it is living its own individuality as a small one, at first it very much picks up on the energy levels of the parents. It is very much aware of what is going on through energy vibration patterns. This goes with you throughout the lifetime as a subliminal belief, so that you have a preconceived tendency to look at life in a certain way.

Later on, when you begin to understand words, your parents may say to you, "It's a jungle out there. You have to be really, really strong. You have to get there first before the other one gets there. Do unto others first before they get you." Or vice versa, "It is really a joyful place to live. I have many friends, you have many friends, nature is beautiful. It is wonderful to be out in the field, to run freely, to feel the sunshine upon the head, the shoulders, the body. It is wonderful to breathe of the fresh air. Life is good."

And so the small one grows taller with beliefs which have been given to him/her early on, and then the beliefs are reinforced as the subliminal belief attracts evidence that the perception is true. And so, ones often will have the challenges in life because they are looking for them, expecting them, because the parents have said, "It's going to be tough; you have to be tough."

Or, the parents will say, "You are going to find many friends. You are a most special being. I prayed before you came, and you came to me to be a companion on the Journey of life, and I am so happy that you came. Let us walk hand in hand and rediscover all of the beauty that this life has to offer."

From that foundation, which is unconscious and yet conscious as well, you fashion how you see your world. You can work with those beliefs when you recognize them. When you sit with yourself just quietly, or when you are traveling in your vehicle or when the mind is free to think back to the childhood or to recognize a re-action to something that happened, stop for a moment; something has happened, and you have a reaction immediately to it, and then there may be a feeling of, "Oh, okay, I know how to handle that," or there is a feeling of, "Oh, my God, how am I going to handle this one?"

You can be aware of how you feel in the body. Stop for a moment and be aware of where you are holding the energy, where it has hit you. Has it hit you at the heart where you feel you have to shut down or can you be open and expansive? Has it hit you in the abdomen, where you feel that you have to be armored and you have to save self?

The torso — from the neck down to below the abdomen — has been oftentimes the part that has been the reason for releasing the body. It has been the area where you were struck in battle; or off with the head, across the neck. So this part of the body is very much attuned to receiving energy, and it will tell you — it has a language — how you are feeling about any occurrence.

Be aware when anything happens, any event, any discourse you have with someone, how you feel about it, where you feel about it, and sit just for a moment in the deep breath, the easy breath, and examine, "What is this telling me about my belief? What do I believe? What am I feeling in the abdomen? What am I feeling anywhere in the body? What energy pattern am I receiving?"

Identify the belief. Oftentimes it will be a belief that says there is something that could be threatening, because habitually as you have gone through this reality many, many lifetimes, you have reinforced a belief that the body which you have fashioned could be harmed in some way. And so there is the initial reaction that perhaps whatever was said to you, whatever occurred could be seen as threatening and could have power of some sort over you.

So you sit with that instantaneous feeling and you ask, "What belief am I holding?" And then you ask, "Where does this come from? What does it go back to?" And there will come to you a vision, an idea, a time, an occurrence, a root source.

And then you ask of yourself, "Is this a belief that serves me now?" Now, in many other lifetimes that belief served you well, because the feeling of threat to the body caused the adrenaline to flow and you ran from whatever was perceived to be threatening, and you did save the body for some other time. And so, that belief and that reaction have served you well. It is not a wrong thing.

But you ask of yourself in this day and time, "Does it serve me now? Do I need this belief now?" If you feel that you do not need it now, you begin by first being conscious of it. Then, secondly, you take a deep breath and you ask, "How can I see this differently?" And as you take that deep breath, you realize that you do not have to hold that belief. There is no parent standing next to you saying that you have to believe it any more. There is no great person in the realms above saying that you have to believe it.

You go within to the energy that you are and you ask of yourself, "How can I see this differently? How would it feel if I understood that what she said to me was said in love?" And you play with that in your imagination. "How would it be if what they said to me was said in love; not as a threat as I first perceived it; not as a judgment as I first perceived it; but when they said that how would it feel if I perceived it said in love?"

You will feel a change in the vibrational energy of the body itself. It will relax. It does not have to be armored any longer. It expands. Every time something comes up and you know, "Oh, that did not feel good," or "Oh, that did feel good," trace it back to what the underlying belief is and be conscious about it.

First of all, be conscious. Second of all, take the deep breath. Third, ask, "How can I see this differently?" And then, fourth, move into the energy feeling of how it feels to perceive it differently. You can do this. You will find yourself being very busy all throughout the day, because truly you go through every day — and this is not said as a judgment, but as a discernment — you go through a day with a lot of reaction to things that you do not even know you are reacting to. You walk through the day half asleep.

I am asking of you now to be awake, to be conscious, to be aware. "What am I feeling? Why am I feeling? What is the underlying belief?" And then if you want to change it, imagine the energy feeling of the opposite: love instead of fear, understanding instead of judgment.

Now, I have spoken to you just now about how to change the conscious beliefs, how to make them conscious and to change. Some beliefs are very deeply embedded in the energy pattern of the body and of the self that you are. They have been very deeply embedded throughout lifetimes. These are ones that are going to be a bit more challenging to find. They are going to be the subconscious ones which will come up as you deal with the ones that are on the surface, the ones of this lifetime.

Other ones from other lifetimes are going to come up to be known. And when I say that, be aware that you have lived many, many lifetimes in many different cultures, so there are going to be beliefs from other cultures that have been taken, integrated, put into the matrix of the soul, and then remembered and carried in the body at the cellular level, so that the cells even have memory of other cultures and other beliefs that those cultures believed in, all the way back as far as you can trace it in a linear history and beyond.

So when ones say to you that belief is a foundation, and that you can change belief, be aware that what you start with is the tip of the iceberg, and that there is much more underneath which will come up at some point.

You all have unique history. You all have unique memories of lifetimes which have been built upon many beliefs, and many of those beliefs are going to be deeply embedded in the energetic pattern of the body. They are accessible to you, but some are just a bit deeper than others. So I say to you, work with the conscious beliefs, the ones that come up in this lifetime that hit you right in the face or right in the stomach, wherever they hit you. Be aware of where that belief comes from. And then give to yourself much allowance and love, because everything you have ever done in any lifetime, even if it has brought to you challenges that you even experience in this lifetime, have been treasures.

You wanted to play in the sandbox of creativity. You have wanted to know, "How does it feel to make sand?" And so you have made plenty of sand. "How does it feel to make the sand castles?" So you make the forms, the bodies. "How does it feel to be finished with one sand castle and to build another?" And so you wipe out one form and you build another sand castle, and you play with that one for awhile.

"How does it feel to throw the sand up in the air? Is it going to stay up in the air?" In some realities it does. In this reality, it comes back down on your head. This reality has much of the sending and receiving, so that what you send out often comes back you. It is part of what you have built into this reality. You have lived every lifetime that you can imagine and more. And many of those lifetimes you have done things that now the energetic pattern of the body does not accept well.

For example, many of the ones who find themselves in this lifetime perceiving the need to avoid the alcoholic substance have come to that place most innocently by the ritual of the religious/philosophical teaching, different threads, different religions as you know them, where the wine was thought to be sacred, and it was imbibed because of the sacredness of it. You were taking something sacred within the body and being One with the energy of that sacred liquid. And those were lifetimes where you were happy. Those were lifetimes where you felt fulfilled. You felt that you were doing something sacred.

Then another lifetime comes along, and you have chosen a different scenario, and you find that you do not feel fulfilled. You want to know fulfillment; you want to know wholeness; and so there is a little part of you that remembers the lifetime where you were in the religious/philosophical order, and what was sacred was the wine. And so you say, "Okay, I will go to the wine. It will make me feel whole."

Perhaps this lifetime the energetic pattern of the body is different, and the wine has a different effect. It is not a sin. It is not wrong; it is a memory, and it goes back to a very good memory, but it may not apply to what you have formed in this lifetime. Therefore, you try it out, and if it resonates well with you, that is good. If it does not, you say, "Okay, that's from another lifetime; it served me in another lifetime, but maybe not this lifetime."

Likewise, there is belief now that the inhalation of smoke is going to bring about a congestion of the lungs, and that eventually you will release the body because it does not feel energetic any longer.

The smoking of the peace pipe was seen as a sacred ritual. There are many of the cultures that yet believe in sharing of the smoke as symbolic of the spirit rising up to the heavens. It was done at first as symbolic catalyst for remembrance. Then ones come through other generational teachings and other lifetimes where the energetic pattern of the body is different, and there is a collective belief that perhaps the smoke can be not sacred, but can be a congestive agent. Again, it is based on a belief.

So when you are working with beliefs, allow yourself much love. Know that truly everything that may not work for you in this lifetime *has* worked for you in other lifetimes and has been seen as a sacred avenue to the remembrance of the spirit that you are, the energy that you are, the divine Isness that you are. But it may not be appropriate for this lifetime, or, it may be.

Have much mercy for yourself, please, and for others as well.

Manifesting Your Desires

Beloved one, I have heard the deepest desires of your heart. You look at your world and it does not seem to reflect back to you the beauty, peace, harmony that you envision in a perfect world. You have individual desires that you wish to see manifest in your life, and separated ego tells you that probably they will not be manifest in the near future, if at all. But I will tell you truly that everything you have desired is happening; it is occurring. That which you have desired to see, to feel, to realize, is in your midst. It is right here already.

It may take you a process of time, as you understand linear time, before you awaken to the realization that, "I already have that which I have been seeking and desiring; I already am that which I have been looking for." So you have what you see to be the nuisance of time, which will call forth the quality, the most wonderful quality, of patience.

You are learning to be at ease with patience, although it is a struggle, and you find yourself from time to time railing against time itself. "Why, after I have put all of this energy into envisioning, looking here and there and everywhere for that which I know will be my fulfillment, why don't I feel fulfilled? Why don't I see it?"

You have in a most wonderful book called *A Course in Miracles* a saying that, "I am determined to see things differently." When you are determined, truly determined, and you practice seeing anew, asking how you can see something differently, the Truth has to be revealed to you. In Truth, you are right in the midst of that which you seek. You are right in the midst of the process – even if you want to call it a process – which brings you to the realization where you then say, "Aha, I have it, and gosh, you know, it has been around me all this time. I have had it all this time."

Many of you are asking to manifest healing of the body, healing of relationships, healing of the employment, healing of aspirations which you want to accomplish in this incarnation. I say unto you, and hear me well, you *are* already doing that which you have desired to do, and you are already that which you have desired to be.

Allow yourself to awaken in the morning, first thing in the morning, and to say, "I know that I am blessed in this day, because my Creator loves me." Your Creator does love you. It has to, because It is Love and you are the extension of Love – and much more than even what the human love can understand. It is Love as Intelligence from before time began; it is Love which goes beyond any human understanding.

You are greatly, greatly loved, and your Creator – which is you, in what you would understand yet to be an expanded Self of you – your Creator does not see any fault, any failing, any lack. You may feel that you do not have everything that you would like to have, that perhaps you do not have the beautiful hair that you would like to have; perhaps you do not have the slimness; or perhaps you do not have the curves of the body that you desire to see; or perhaps you do not have the employment you would desire; or perhaps there is a quality of personality that you would like to feel. Perhaps the world around you seems to reflect only chaos and tragedy, with no purpose.

However, if you will hear me truly, everything works together in divine perfect order. Everything works to bring you to that place of awakening where you say, "I Am the awakened Christ. I Am already that which I have wanted to be. I Am already the knowledgeable master. I thought I had to read about it in a book. I thought I had to attend a hundred and one workshops; workshops that were not just an hour long, but the workshops had to be weekend workshops, or perhaps a week; they had to be of a certain length of time so that we could actually get into, in depth, understanding about things, and I had to do a hundred and one of these. A hundred was not enough; I had to do one more before I would be the knowledgeable master."

Well, I say unto you as I have said many times, you are already the master who is bringing forth all of the workshops; not for the purpose of *learning* anything more—you already know it – but to allow yourself to be in concert with others of like mind and to be there for them as they feel that they have to keep seeking; to say to them, "I like you just the way you are."

That is why you go to the workshops; to be with others of like mind and to share the vibration of like-mindedness, of love and of acceptance; to know that truly you are loved with a greater love than you can ever, ever imagine.

Take that deeply within the consciousness and allow yourself to feel. "How does it feel to know that I am loved with a love that is greater than I can even imagine? I am the little Child, the little girl who ran in the sunshine and wanted to know more. I am the little boy who was always asking questions, always asking, 'Why?' I am still that little girl, that little boy."

And you are, because that Child of you is always within you; the holy Child of you. As you grow taller, you put on a certain persona that you think the world will accept, yet the little Child of you is still wanting to be acknowledged and to be loved. That is why you listen to my voice within your mind and heart, to know how truly loved you are; to feel it; not just to read the words, but to feel how it feels to live in the kingdom of love itself; to be the little Child and to know that truly you are always loved, taken care of, nurtured, as you want to be taken care of and nurtured.

Then you can take that deep breath, and no matter what the world will bring to you, you know that you do not walk your path alone. You walk it with love. You walk with friends, ones that you can see, and you walk it with friends that are unseen, because truly, as we have said so many times, there is no separation.

The ones that you do not see with the physical eyes – your guides, your teachers, your guardian angels, your loved ones who have passed from your sight – they are with you always. They cheer you on. They listen to you as you rant and rave, and they smile, because they know what truly you are: the small child in the sandbox throwing the sand up in the air and then wondering, "Why does the sand come down on top of me?" They watch this, and they know that at some point in time you are going to stop for a moment and there is going to be a peace which will descend rather than sand, and you are going to realize, "Oh, I am the one who is throwing all the sand and dust up around me, all of this chaos. Ha! I was doing it. How great I am."

And then you change, because there is new perception, there is new understanding of how powerful you are, how you create everything; not for the purpose of suffering; not even for the purpose of learning; but you create everything for the purpose of seeing the love in it, because everything is a gift of love to you. Everything.

Then the awakened Christ – which is you – says, "How good it is to be alive," whether you are functioning with a body or not. "How good it is to be alive." Your loved ones, as they have released the body and have felt themselves to be free of having to drag the dust of our holy Mother, the Earth, around and have felt themselves to be free, and yet alive, have said, "How good it is to be alive." And how surprised they are sometimes, "I am still alive!" How freeing that acknowledgment is.

There is a little-known secret of manifesting which is not a secret, but has yet to be realized: "I am already manifesting that which I desire. I have only to change my perception a small bit."

Everything truly is unfolding according to a plan that you set in motion as time began, and when the purpose of time is fulfilled, the awakened Christ will say, "Hey, that was really a fun experience we had; over and over and over, you know? Sometimes I had to play that role many times before I really knew it. I would miss some of the lines, so I had to go back to play that role over and over, and play it with different actors and actresses to see how it felt to play it with different nuances."

Ask yourself now, "What do I truly desire? What do I really want to manifest?" Become really clear about what you want to manifest, and then look around. Perhaps you already have it; maybe not in the form that you were expecting it to be, but you have it.

Ask yourself, first of all, "What do I truly desire to manifest?" Then ask yourself, "Why do I want to manifest that? What is the underlying reason that I feel that something may be lacking?" Because always if you want to manifest something, the underlying thinking is that you do not already have it.

So get very clear about why you want to manifest it. "What is the underlying motivation? What is it that I feel is not right or whole that needs to be changed?"

Three steps bring the awakened Christ into joy. "What do I truly want to manifest? Why do I want to manifest it? What is the underlying motivation, the underlying fear that something could be not quite whole or not quite all there?" Take the deep breath, and then realize that truly you already have it. You already *are* it.

"What do I desire? Why do I desire? I do have it." That is the secret side of manifesting.

Now, you have many, many workshops; many, many books; many, many tapes, CD's, electronic recordings that tell you how to manifest, but they forget the last part, to tell you that you already have it. Even if they ask you the second part of why do you want to manifest it, oftentimes you do not go deep enough into that to understand that truly it comes from a fear that you do not have it or that you are not good enough to have it.

When you get to the place of identifying the fear or the reason why you feel that you have to have this desire to be made manifest and you get really clear about that, you laugh, because you realize you have come to the very root of everything that has ever been bothering you. You come to the very root of whatever you have been, in any time, in any lifetime wanting to manifest, out of seeming lack. Then you realize, "I am the awakened Christ. I am already that which I have been seeking. That which I thought I was seeking was falsely predicated on a belief that I didn't have it or that I wasn't good enough or that somehow someone else had it and I didn't have it." But you already are and you already have, and if you want to make any changes, allow yourself to make the changes.

Separated ego then speaks to you, "You'd better watch out, because in this world you make no changes without giving up something; it's always a trade, and you may not want this trade. Now, make sure before you make this change that you are not getting into something worse."

But if you know already that you *are* whole, complete, awakened, knowledgeable, rich, abundant, then it really does not matter whether you stay here or you go there, because you are going to be Who you are wherever you are. Manifesting is going to bring you many opportunities to see things differently. The world often seems to present chaos, both in general and sometimes closer to home. You are going to have many opportunities, not only for challenges, but for joy and friendship.

Whenever the world is too much with you, remember to take the deep breath, and ask yourself the three secret questions of manifesting: "What do I truly desire to manifest? Why do I want to manifest it? What is the underlying motivation?" Then be determined to see things differently.

Beloved one, you do not have to struggle any longer. You are that which you desire to manifest.

Unlimited Possibilities

Beloved one, this is a most exciting time. We have spoken for some years of the excitement of the changes that are happening. We have spoken of what to expect, and you have found out that my timing is not your timing, and some of you have been most impatient with timing. But truly, you are beginning to see, as you will cast your mind back in time, how everything in your life and in the collective consciousness has been bringing you to this point in time and in reality.

Truly, every day is a new opportunity for experiences. We have said to you that before you put the feet on the floor and get out of the bed in the morning, spend one moment visualizing how you want that day to go. Who are you going to meet in that day? How are you going to feel about them? Allow yourself to walk in holy Light. Visualize the holy Light going before you. Allow yourself to see yourself and everyone else you meet in that day in holy Light.

As you can set the tone for each day even before you begin the day, you can do that for the week, for the month. Visualize this month how you want it to go, where you want it to go, where you want to go, even physically where you want to go, who you want to interact with, and take off all of the boundaries of what separated ego has said could be possible.

I have given you small pieces of homework from time to time: to write down options, ideas, and see how you feel about the idea. You will know what you want to do. There will be a feeling registering in the body as to whether you want to do that or not. You will not need to run off to your experts and ask them, "Should I do this? What does my future look like?"

No one else can tell you your future. They can tell you possibilities. They can even tell you probabilities based on what you have chosen in the past, but they cannot tell you your future, because only you can make the choices. That is why I do not say to you, "This is what is going to happen" in black and white.

It bothers some of the brothers and sisters, because they would like definitive answers in black and white. But I cannot give that to you, because I am not walking in your sandals. I am not living your life. I walk *with* you. I walk *within* you as the divine expression of holy energy, Intelligence, but I cannot say in the next moment what you are going to choose to do.

Your news media loves to bring you options for your choosing. Your news media is very good at doing that. The ones who pay money to have their product on the various news media channels want to have your attention, and they have found in the past that what gets your attention is drama, tragedy, calamity or possible calamity.

But, beloved one, that is not *all* that is happening in the world. There are many, many places where there is love of brother and sister, where there are miracles happening, miracles of healing on all levels that do not get reported because they are not of the big drama.

I have said to you many times that there will be drama, wars and rumors of war always in your world, but that is not the Truth of your being. I have said to you, if you want to heal something, any situation, it is to see first the appearance; you do not deny that that is happening in the world; but then you pray and you fast.

Everything that happens in the world can be healed by prayer and fasting. Now, prayer means to contemplate what is happening from the highest point of view, to know the holiness of the situation. Allow yourself to be the angelic being that truly you are and to look down, as it would be, upon the drama that is happening and to see it as small children playing in the sandbox who, after a time, will get tired of that game and will want to come out of the sandbox to see what is beyond it.

Prayer is the beholder, the perspective from the highest point of view. Fasting does not mean in the physical sense that you do not eat. It means that you take your attention away from what seems to be happening and you see the truth without any emotion. Allow yourself to withdraw the emotion. You fast from being drawn into the drama, into the appearance of anything other than the Truth of each one's Being.

You have a saying in your world which is most wonderful: to accentuate the positive. Look upon the positive. When your news media brings you all of the news of the doom and gloom, how there is war, how there is inhumanity, how there are hard times economically, how many of the brothers and sisters are suffering because they have lost their jobs…in truth, they never owned that job. Sometimes it owned them, and sometimes it is better for them to move on.

So, in truth, it is all a blessing, even though separated ego is going to scream, yell, and kick its feet up in the air, pound on the floor having a temper tantrum. But you know what happens with the temper tantrum? If you have ever watched a small one—or a big one—with a temper tantrum, if you do not try to rescue that one in the middle of a temper tantrum—and I advise you not to, because it is a bit dangerous—after the temper tantrum energy has spent itself, there is a peace that descends, a peace that allows that one then to see things differently.

It is at that point, a most blessed point, where you turn within and you acknowledge, "I AM. I am divine Intelligence expressing and experiencing life. How do I want it to be?"

Allow yourself to move forward in confidence. If you are one of the ones who is making a transition in employment, count it all as good. Get very busy doing your small bit of homework writing down, "Where would I like to be? Where would I like to spend my time and receive in exchange the golden coins, or perhaps the chicken or the grain?"

There used to be not so much of the golden coins or the paper. It used to be more of the exchange. The collective consciousness is getting back to that now. "What do I have in my house—literally and figuratively, metaphysically—what do I have that I can share with others?" All of you have hope that you can share with other ones. All of you have a knowing of who the brothers and sisters are, that they are not just what they have envisioned themselves to be as the body or as the employment would dictate. That is not who they are.

Share. That is the blessed knowing of abundance: where ones share with each other, not hoarding, not like some of the ones who are now coming to light who have had the golden parachutes, and they are finding that the gold in those parachutes is weighing them down. They are not being lighter than air. They are coming crashing down, because the gold in that parachute is too heavy.

You have in the collective consciousness a most wonderful interdependence which is truly proving to you the Oneness of the divine holy Child. It has yet to be recognized, but that is what is coming forth. The interdependence now is seen to be a bit shaky. It is called your economic system. And as you have discerned, your economic system has been built upon belief, confidence in the system, and when the confidence starts to drain away, it is as the house of cards that begins to fall.

Your economic system is built upon confidence. There has been a wise one recently who has spoken out and has said, "If you have abundance, spend it." If you have the golden coins, if you have the employment right now, spend it. Put the golden coins into circulation—that is truly what they are meant to do: to circulate, and to believe that there will always be more, because there *will* always be more.

The loss of confidence is as a downward spiral, and you are the ones, and the friends that you talk to are the ones who can change that spiral and make it go back up again. It is easy to do once you change your thinking.

Economics has always been built on having confidence in "what I have and what I have to share," for you know that you are abundant. You know that you have the material goods. And more than that, you have what cannot be touched by the dust or the moth; it cannot rot. You have within you the wisdom and the most precious gift of all, the gift of hope, to give and to share with other ones.

You have the most precious gift of confidence—a most wonderful word. We have spoken many times of the clues that are within your words. Confidence, meaning "with faith". Con—"with"—fidence—"faith". When you go with faith, confidently, and you say, "I know that always I am going to be taken care of; I know that I have an abundance, and I will spend freely what I have," then it spreads to another one and another one.

Allow your confidence to be contagious. Let someone else catch it. Allow yourself to spend, to buy, to share the golden coins, because always there will be more. There has to be. You are the creators of wealth. You have created it in the first place. And as you allow it to flow through you, as you have the confidence that there is going to be more, there will be more; always there will be more.

You have unlimited possibilities. Which ones of the unlimited possibilities are you going to make into probabilities? Look at the ones that you have written down or the ones you have mentally put on your list and you have said, "Oh, that one really appeals to me. I want to do that one. I'll make that one a probability. Probably in this year I will travel. I will find a place to share my love. Probably in this year that which I have been working on for a lifetime will come to be manifest."

Make it a probability. It is right now a possibility, but as you work with it, as you live with it, as you have the confidence to know that it can be—and I assure you that it can be, and I have that on good assurance—you make it a probability. When you sit with that probability and it becomes part of you, then it becomes a reality.

If you feel that there are blockages to what you would like to do, if you feel that you are in a fog about what to do, do not fight the fog. Let it be there. It is as a nurturing mist. Go within and ask of yourself, "How do I want this year to unfold? What do I want to do in this year? I am my Father's Child. I am the extension—not only the Child that would speak yet of separation—but I am the extension of divine Intelligence. I can make all things new."

If you are tired of the old and you want to make change, begin by asking, "Okay, how can I make a step in that direction? Who do I have to talk to? How do I talk to them? Who will help me with this, perhaps," because sometimes you feel that you are a solitary point of Light and you want others to affirm with you that which you want, and there is power in a grouping that is affirming the same thing.

Ask and you shall receive, but you have to ask first. That has to come first, and it helps if you have some clarity about what you are asking; otherwise, you may get a whole drawer full of trinkets that are beautiful, each one in its own right, but what are you going to choose out of this drawer full of trinkets? So have a bit of clarity and ask, and then go forward with confidence. Have confidence in your economics. In truth, there is no lack. There are as many of the golden coins, there is as much of the wealth now as there was six months ago, a year ago, ten years ago. It is getting redistributed, yes, but there is as much.

When you have confidence in the economic system, when you know you do not have to hoard, you do not have to worry about the morrow, you begin to remember Who you are. Consider the lilies of the field. They do not worry, "Is it going to rain tomorrow? Is the sun going to shine tomorrow? Is the wind going to be gentle, or is it going to be strong and blow me over?"

Consider the lilies. They express what they are. They have confidence in their being.

If you want to buy something, buy it. Use the golden coins the way they were meant to be—in circulation.

Let others think that perhaps you are foolhardy. Ah, but you are a happy fool. Go joyfully, full of confidence. Act "as if…" and it will be.

Dreams and Desires

Let us speak now about dreams and desires, the nighttime dreams and their messages, yes, but more than that I would speak with you about the dreams that you have as goals of something you want to see made manifest.

All of you have dreams of what you would like to see happening in your future, and you spend some of your time in the daytime with the daydreams as you envision what you would like to see manifest and what you would like to experience. This is very good, because it allows your point of focus to expand and to play, truly, with your divinity; to play with the unlimitedness that you are.

How would it feel if you could move into one of the unlimited possibilities of the daydream? How would it feel if all of the limitations were taken off; what would you dream; how would you be? Daydreams are important.

Desire is what activates and brings into manifest form the daydream. As we have spoken many times, your words hold clues for you. Examine your words. Be aware of what words you choose.

The word "desire" truly is from "de" "sire"—of the Father. Therefore, your desires do come from the Father. Be awake to your desires. Be awake to your daydreams. Be awake to the power of the imagination. Imagination is a tool, a gift that you put into this reality so that you could play with the possibility of taking limitations off and being, manifesting that which you would like to see in your daydreams and in your desire.

When you bring the two together, when you bring the daydream into alignment with desire, desire puts the energy into the daydream to make it happen. When it is of the

Father, when it is of your divinity and is of your divine path, then the daydream manifests. There is nothing that can hold it back.

So start first with the daydream. Whenever you get time to daydream, think of what you would like to see in your future and what you would like to see manifest in the world. Then ask, "Is this in alignment with my divine Self and the divine Self of others? Is it of the Father?"

Sometimes you will have to examine and go very deeply within yourself to see where the daydream comes from, to see, "Why do I want to see this dream come true? Is it based on ego that wants to make manifest something that others will then praise me for? Or, is it based on fear that if I don't realize this dream, something really disastrous might happen? Or, is it based on limited thinking?"

That may be a tough one as you go deeply within yourself, because limited thinking has been a gift that generations have given over and over to the younger generations. It is the voice that says, "Well, this would be nice, but it probably can't happen."

So go deeply within yourself and ask, "Where does this dream come from? Why do I want to manifest this?" Play with all of the parameters of the daydream. Play with, "How would it feel?"

Play for a minute or so with "what if". "What if the limited thinking isn't true? What if I can manifest the dream in alignment with desire? What if?"

For example, what if you truly live in a friendly universe, and all of the stories of your ETs have been based on the belief, which *this* reality holds, that there is good and that there is opposition to good? This reality, as we have said many times, is based upon a belief in duality, that there is good and that there is evil, but what if this reality is only *one* sandbox, only one place to play, and there are many other sandboxes that do not believe in duality?

What if all of your stories about the universe, about how ETs are going to have more power than you do, how they are going to come and overtake you, are not true? Some of your Hollywood stories like to bring you a lot of drama. What if there is intelligence beyond this one planet, and what if that intelligence is a positive intelligence, friendly intelligence?

What if it is a friendly universe? What if all of the stories that you have ever been told are just that, stories? You love stories. You love drama. You love to play with the adrenaline rush. After all, it makes you feel alive. If you are in a certain place of fear or drama and the adrenaline is flowing, you know yourself to be totally alive.

So when you have a dream of something you want to see made manifest, go into it deeply. What would it look like? What would it feel like? And yes, it is going to change as you play with it, because the boundaries of the dream that you have are going to be a bit fluid. You are going to think, "Well, it's going to have such and such qualities," and then you say, "Well, maybe more like…." And then that suggests to you something different.

The mind is going to be very busy. The imagination is going to be very busy. Then there is going to come a time when the heart will be in alignment with the mind, and then you will know that the dream has come into alignment with desire. The heart will tell you that it feels right.

Many of you have been brought up with teachings from the parents and from the peers and from the "authoritative ones" who thought, or at least gave you the impression, that they knew what was best for you. When you were small, you accepted what they gave you, because you, for survival's sake, found that it was probably best to go along.

However, as the years have gone by, you have said, "Perhaps they weren't as right as they thought they were. Perhaps I know what is best for me, better than anyone else," and you do, because you are the one who is walking in your sandals.

No one else, well-meaning as they may be, can tell you how it feels to walk in your sandals. No one else, even I or other ascended masters, can tell you what is best for you, but you will know it when the mind and heart come into alignment, when you come to that place when the dream of what you hope can be comes to the place of knowing, "It is."

When you bring the dream of what you want to see manifest and what you want to experience into the place of understanding, "I already have it," then the heart allows you to send it back to the mind to do the technical working out of what the structure is going to be.

Hear me well. When you come to the realization of the fact that you already have that dream – in potential — then the heart sends the message back to the mind—because the mind is the servant of the heart—"How now do we make this manifest? What are the technicalities of it? What does the structure look like? What do I have to do? What is the first step?"

If you are asking for healing of the body, know that truly you already have it. Then allow the mind to direct you to go to certain facilitators, certain nutritional ways which can be, in the outer, helpful. But know that, first of all in the heart, you already have healing of the body. It is already done. Then the mind, as I have said, will direct you with certain guidance to go and speak with certain ones, and you follow whatever they may offer to you if it feels in resonance with what would be healing for you.

As you bring your dreams into alignment with the heart, into alignment where the desire of the Father knows the next step, you are going to have the most miraculous—according to the world—experiences.

Right now you have evidence that the Intelligence of the universe is making itself felt in ways that cannot be explained by your present-day technology. You have the most wondrous crop circles that are being made all over our holy Mother Earth; not by man, because men have tried to replicate and have found that it is not the same. And it is not happening just in one place, because if it were just limited to one place, then your scientists would come up with an explanation for it, or at least they would try.

But it is happening all over the planet in different places, and the designs are most intricate. The designs truly are a language that evokes a remembrance, albeit seemingly far away from present day awareness, but a language that you know. You look at them and you cannot read them, but it is the same with many of your languages in this day and time.

There are many languages. Do you know how to read Russian? Do you know how to read Greek? There are many languages you look at and they are squiggles; beautiful squiggles. Some of the Aramaic writings are beautiful squiggles, but what do they mean?

So you look upon the crop circles and you say, "These designs are beautiful, but I don't know what they mean." There will come a time when there will be an "Aha!" — a sort of Rosetta Stone which will explain what the crop circle designs mean.

There will be ones who will have the night-time dreams where they get up in the morning and they have written something that does not quite make sense in the language that you are accustomed to. But in time, in the exquisite right timing, that writing is going to decode the crop circles. It is already in process.

That is why I say unto you, recognize that you already have it. Any dream that you would make manifest, look around you and say, "I already have it; now show it to me." That is the next question separated ego is going to say. "Well, okay, if I already have it and it already exists, show it to me."

If you have any dream, if you have any desire that you have been working with this lifetime or other lifetimes—because you have come into this lifetime carrying with you dreams, hopes, visions of wanting to know Home right here in this human experience—those visions are going to be coming more and more into your awareness.

Already you have the feeling that, "I want to be free. I want to know the power of being invulnerable, the power of being totally free. I don't want to feel at the mercy of someone else's choices and dictates. I want to live in the present right now."

The past has seemed to dictate what you have to be in the present, but in truth, the past is not real. It is not with you, except as you bring it into this reality. The past, where is it? In memory only. That is why we have said to you in other times, if there have been experiences in your past that have not been loving, that have not been the kind that would allow you to feel good about yourself, you can go back and change those memories.

Any experience: perhaps when you were small and you did not understand the ways of the world and you did not understand what the parents wanted and they were harsh, judgmental, abusive with you, you can go back to that memory, get right back into it, feel it, and then change it.

Recognize, first of all, that they were not seeing you. They did not see *you*. They were reacting to their own perception of what they thought you were, what you were doing, what they had to do. They were reacting to old perceptions that had been handed down to them by their parents, generation unto generation, and they did not truly see you.

If they had seen you, as the angelic being that you are, if they had seen you as the Light and the love that you are, the loving little one who wanted only to please, they would not have struck out. But they did not see you. Their perception was the perception molded by their experiences of what they had learned from their parents and from society at that time, of what they thought they had to do.

So you can go back to that memory—and there may be many of those memories—and you can change each one with the wave of your magic wand of asking, "Where is the past? It no longer exists except as I bring it into the present."

That is how powerful you are. That is why you are not limited to the present. You are not limited even to what you see the future to be. You are going to make your own future by the power of changing your perceptions. Hear that well. You are going to make your future according to how you change your *perceptions*.

That is why there is a saying in one of the books that I authored, "I am determined to see things differently. I desire to see things anew." How can you see things anew? How would this be if it were different in your perception?

I love that which you are, because you are love itself. Nothing else exists. Separated ego will give you a lot of drama to play with, but that is what it is—drama, a story, something to play with. It is as sand in the sandbox. You can throw the past, the drama, the hurts up in the air and allow the wind to take them away. They are gone.

Always I will love you, because I know that which you are: the innocent holy Child, come to play in a harsh sandbox.

Allow yourself the dreams. Ask of the dream, "What does this truly mean? Where is the desire in resonance with the dream?" Know that you already have it, and allow the exquisite right timing for the dream to be made manifest.

What Are You Waiting For?

Beloved one, you have been born into a world that believes in duality and focuses quite often upon the heaviness of what possibly might go wrong and what probably will go wrong, as the world sees it. Your news media is very experienced at bringing you the worst that possibly could be — and sometimes a little bit of good news just so they will not be criticized as being one-sided. But they are heavily weighted to bring you the heavy-weighted material. Now, there is experience that is going on in the world that *is* seemingly of tragedy and inhumanity, and it does not take too much looking in order to find it, but there is also the Light and lightheartedness if you want to and will allow yourself to look for it. It is there.

You can find things in your life that you think could be a bit better, but if you focus upon those, always you will be in a place of wanting to make better, and you will be ignoring that which truly is harmonious and good in your life. So focus on the good. Focus on your power, the divine power, the power of choice, for in every moment you have power which no one can take from you.

You have the power of choice as to where you will abide; whether you are going to stay in a place of, "Woe is me; look at all of the challenges that I have; look at all of the possible things that could go wrong," or, "Wow, this is really great. Look what I am manifesting for myself."

Your power lies in the power of choice. Everything every moment is a choice as to how you will feel, how you will perceive things, how you will want things to be in the next moment or so. You are powerful. The world will say unto you that there is much to be guarded against, much that you have to watch out for. But in every moment you have the power of choice, the power to say "No" to whatever might come to threaten your peace. You have the power to say "No, I'm not going to stay in the place of heaviness, the place that feels like it is a casket. I'm going to arise up and live this life in the way I would like it to be, even if it seems, at first, like it would be a fairy tale and I cannot really live it that way."

You *can,* because a lifetime is made up of choices, one by one by one. And truly, each choice, when you choose either to be down or you choose to be up, leads to the next choice and makes the next choice easier. So if you keep choosing heaviness and fear, guess what the next choice is going to be. However, if you choose lightness and possible happiness – even if it feels like you are pretending — it is going to be much easier to choose for joy in the next moment.

The world at large, the collective, is undergoing much of a shift in perspective. And so, with the new energy that you are bringing forth, you as a collective people, you are rising up and demanding change, and it is happening.

You have now groups of people springing up to focus their light upon the inequities that have been in the old paradigm. Every day you will find news of a new focal point where there can be new light upon situations that have been swept under the carpet for a long, long time.

There is much power that you individually and collectively are taking back. For a long time you felt yourself to be under the thumb of political authorities, religious/philosophical authorities, and others who had more of the golden coins. You felt yourself to be under their thumb, because they seemingly had more worldly power and you were not awakened to your own individual power and your own collective power as you group together.

You are awakening, finally, once again, because truly the awakening happens in a cycle of time. There is a harvesting that happens, where the seeds are planted and you go through lifetimes, individually and collectively, where the seeds germinate and there is new thinking.

So you have harvested—ascended in your knowing; I use the word harvested as the same as ascension—you have taken what you have experienced in lifetimes and, as you have understood those lifetimes, you have moved to a higher vibration, a higher understanding of yourself and who you are and who others are and why things are happening.

My question to you now is, "What are you waiting for?" Why are you waiting for some future time for the ascension in consciousness to be claimed? Why not have it on the morrow? If you have it in your conscious plan to know peace and love and to project out that vision, why wait?

If you have an idea of what you want to see manifest, why wait? Are you waiting for a savior to come and make everything right? Well, the savior is already here. You are your own savior.

I am not going to come down, as has been foretold in some of your religious/philosophical teachings, in a chariot of white light and say, "You and you and you and you, come with me. The rest of you, you have more work to do." It is not going to happen that way.

You are your own savior as you make choice to be your own savior, as you make choice to say, "Wow, I'm much more than I ever thought I was. I thought I was just human." Well, that is part of you, and it is a blessed part of you, the human experience, but it is not all of who you are.

You can wait if you want to. But why wait? Are you waiting until all of the collective gets its act together? Well, that may take a little longer. It may take quite a bit longer, because there are still ones who want a human experience and want to know completion with every nuance of the human experience, and that may take them some more lifetimes. But does that mean that you have to hang around and suffer with them?

If you go down in the pit with them and play their game, where are you at that point? You are down in the pit. Does that help them rise up? No. It only adds more credence to what they have thought to be true: that life is meant to be suffering. Better you should stay up out of the pit, and if they choose to be in the pit for awhile or they choose to play games, let them play their games, but what is that to you?

Choose thou where you will be. Choose thou me. There is a quotation in your Scriptures that runs something like that, which means to choose to know your divine nature, the Christ, to know good, happiness, appreciation of all the blessings in your life, and not to be down in the pit. Or if you find yourself falling into the pit once in awhile, you have your divine ladder; climb back up out of the pit.

What are you waiting for? "Well, I don't have enough of the golden coins. I have this vision of what I want to do; I have a trip that I would love to make to a foreign land to see if there are brothers and sisters there who are of like mind, but I don't have the golden coins for that." And you never will if you are going to focus on the lack. Start with what you have; start putting away the golden coins—it is called saving. As you put the focus upon what you have, it multiplies.

"Well, I'm not as young as I used to be. I don't think I can actually do this project. Maybe ten years ago I could have, but now I think it's passed me by." Well, as long as you take breath into the body, you can do anything you want to do, no matter how many years the calendar says you have had. As long as you are breathing, you can do, go, accomplish whatever you are desiring to do.

"I'm not going to be able to go back to school and learn a new trade. The world wouldn't allow me into a school because I'm too old or I don't have the right qualifications." How about using your wonderful technology for on-line courses and the networking of the Internet?

"Well, I can't do it because my family wouldn't like it if I did this. They wouldn't understand, and they would criticize me." What is that to you? Oftentimes you choose the biological family in order to sandpaper some of the rough edges off of yourself. You have wondered sometimes, "Why did I choose to be born into a family that doesn't understand me? I feel more in a family when I'm with ones of like mind."

You often choose your biological family for the sandpapering. So you can look at them and you can say, "Thanks; you did a really good job of sandpapering. I didn't realize I had that rough spot, but you've really polished it, and sometimes it hurt, but now it's been polished, and now I have found my true family, the ones of like mind, the ones I can rejoice with."

So what are you waiting for? Are you waiting for someone else to give you permission? Well, I am going to take that excuse away from you. I give you permission as of right now to do whatever you have hoped, dreamed, wanted to do in this lifetime. I give you permission to feel free to choose happiness, to feel free to create that which is pleasant. I give you permission.

Whatever you want to do, follow the inner guidance. That is truly your strength: the power of choice to follow your inner guidance. If something does not feel right for you, it is 99 percent of the time due to timing. It is not that the dream, the hope, the vision is wrong, but it has to do with timing. So, as I have said many, many times to you, "Patience."

Cultivate the strength of patience. Know that all is in your divine order. Everything is unfolding for the best. If you have felt that you have been held back from doing something, allow yourself to understand the gift of timing. You have built the gift of time into this reality, as a nuisance sometimes, but also as a safety net.

Listen to your inner guidance and ask of yourself, "What am I waiting for?" It may be timing. Use a bit of common sense along with the impulsiveness of creativity to fashion for yourself the very best outcome.

What are you waiting for? Be clear about what you are waiting for. Maybe what you are waiting for is staying in the future because there is yet something that you want to complete where you are.

Sometimes what you are waiting for is the timing, and one of the most difficult challenges is to have a vision, to want to get on with it, to know the creativity, to know you have the power to do it, and then to acquiesce to the higher self of timing and to be patient and to trust. But while you are waiting and while you are trusting, start working with positive attitude, start putting aside some of the savings, start changing the thinking so that when the timing *is* right, you can move ahead quickly.

Sometimes there is disappointment because the vision or situation does not come as quickly as you would like it to. Sometimes you look back over the years and you say, "Well, all those ideas I had a decade ago, two decades ago, well, they were great ideas, but they didn't happen." It does not mean that they are not going to happen. The important thing is to know patience, to know trust, and to begin as if you were going to move right into that vision on the morrow, and get the energy amped up so that when the timing *is* right, you and anyone else who may be working with you will be ready to move quickly ahead and manifest.

There is a divine timing about everything, and that is very challenging in world issues, in the reality of the world, because seemingly you have to be in concert with others pulling the cart up the mountainside, all pulling together. In Truth, you are. There is an evolutionary shift that is taking place, and you *are* all pulling the cart up the mountainside together, even though it may look like many are pulling it backwards. In Truth, you are making progress with it.

In Truth, the shift has already become visible. You can see some of the changes that are happening: more focus upon respect for all living beings, more light upon issues that have been hidden, more courage to question old ways of thinking. So take heart from what you can see, and then trust that what is unseen is unfolding as it must in the divine plan.

That is why I have spoken to you so often about being the beholder, being able to step back from whatever seemed to be so close to you that you could not see the Big Picture. Watch the drama, watch the choices, and see how everything does work together for the atonement, the realization of at-One-ment.

Every moment you have choice. Make your choices with awareness. Make your choice with trust and patience if the timing does not seem quite right. Follow the inner prompting that you have, because it comes from your Self.

Nothing is ever done by chance; it is all by divine plan. So ask of yourself, "What am I waiting for? Is it for someone else to tell me to go ahead? Or am I waiting because my inner guidance tells me that I should wait?" Listen to what it is telling you. Amp up the energy. Believe. Trust. Have patience as you keep the vision alive. No vision, dream, idea comes to you without purpose. And if you cannot do Omega, Sigma, Theta right now, then do Alpha, Beta, Delta while you are waiting. Above all, make your waiting pleasant, awakened, happy, excited, and trusting.

The Secret of Receiving

I would speak with you now about something that is dear to your heart: the secret of receiving. You have been asking to manifest; asking, with the palms open, saying, "Okay, I am asking; I am ready; I want it, but since I don't see it yet, there must be a secret to it."

Everyone loves a secret. It is something special. It is something shared just among friends. It is something that perhaps not everybody knows, and it makes you special if you know the secret. In truth, the secret of receiving is very simple. But it does have a catch to it, and we will come to that later.

The secret of receiving is to know that truly already you have it. There is nothing outside of you. It is all within you and all within your power to bring it forth. The secret of receiving – as I have said, and it is recorded in your holy Scriptures – is to pray unto the Father/Mother, pray believing that you have received. *Know* that you have received, and then it will appear right in front of you, right in the midst of where you are.

Pray believing; in other words, whatever you are asking for, look around you and realize you already have it. Now, perhaps the world will speak to you that, yes, you have the potential of it, but you have not brought it forth yet. But in truth, you *are* bringing it forth even as you think to manifest. Even as you think to receive, you are bringing it forth with that vision, and the more you think about it and the more clarity you have about it, the easier it is to recognize that truly you already have it and you already have the means to be in awareness that you have it.

This is where friends come in, good friends who are in resonance with you; not friends who are of the questioning kind, but friends who are of like mind. The friends you share your dreams with and who are in resonance with you can often point out to you that what you are asking for, you do already have; perhaps not in the way you have been looking at it from one angle or maybe from another angle, but you already have it.

So when you pray, pray with the vision of what you want to see in the outer. Go first to the inner, with the inner vision, and acknowledge that, "That which I am asking for, I truly already have. I am wealthy beyond any measure of what the world will say."

Oftentimes you are tricked into thinking that you need a certain number of golden coins or certain numbers in your bank account in order to be able to do what you want to do. But I say unto you that if, for example, you wanted to go to a far country and it was going to cost you a lot of the golden coins and you were thinking, "I can't do that because I don't have the golden coins," you find a way to manifest a discount or you find a friend who needs a companion, or you find a friend who will lend you the golden coins so that you can get where you want to go. You always find a creative way to manifest that which is your dream, your vision.

So as you pray, believing, and you allow the eyes, even the physical eyes to see that you are in the midst of that which you have desired and you know that that which you have been asking for, you already have, there comes a great sense of gratitude. "I am truly blessed" – and you are – "with what I do have."

I would set for you a piece of homework: sit down with a piece of paper and a pen, and take stock of what you do have. You will be surprised, because you will fill pages of the notebook with what you do have, even down to the smallest little thing. You will start out with the big things first, and then you will add more to it, and more, and maybe the next day you will come back and you will add a couple more things to the list, and before you know it, you are going to be living in great gratitude because, "Look at how wealthy I am. Look at what I have to be thankful for. Look at what I have that is freely given to me, things that I do not even have to have responsibility for. I don't have to expend any energy to have these things. They are already mine to enjoy." Everything you desire, you are already creating for yourself.

Sometimes you create what appear to be bumps in the road in the journey of a lifetime, but oftentimes the bumps in the road are the most wonderful gifts that you can give to yourself. Later when you look back, you say, "If that bump or that wall, or whatever, wasn't there, I wouldn't have made the turn which has brought me here."

The secret to receiving is to know, first of all, that you have already received. The secret to receiving is to stand in gratitude because you have already received and you are already in the midst of receiving.

Furthermore, the secret to receiving is to be willing to give. That is what I said is the catch, but it is not a big catch. It is an easy catch. In order to receive, you have to be willing to give; in other words, to let everything flow through you; to know that, "I am unlimited; I have all the resources that I can ever think of or desire or would ask for, and I share them with you."

As you share them with another friend, they are multiplied as they flow through you, and you are then the receiver who has tenfold of what you are giving out to another one, and you become aware, even more aware of what you already are and have, because you are able to give it. You cannot give it if you do not have it. True? Even the world teaches you that.

Then the world shifts and changes because of your willingness to be the giver. As you allow the giving to flow through you, you realize, "I can give and give and give and give, and more will be given unto me as I give." The gratitude grows, and you get out the notebook and you start writing some more things in the notebook because you realize, "As I give, it is repaid in the flow ten times, multiplied tenfold as I give it out to others;" tenfold because you realize that you are living in an unlimited spirit of the I Am-ness, the Creative One that you are.

The ultimate secret to receiving is to give, and to give freely, over and over and over and over; to actually get quite busy in making an inventory of, "What can I give?" As you wake up in the morning every day, before you put the feet upon the floor, think about what you want to give away in that day, be it tangible or intangible.

Think about the wealth that you have to give, and then get busy giving it away, because the more you give, the more that will come right back to you. You have heard the saying, "Nature abhors a vacuum." Well, spirit is like that, too. There never is a vacuum. Whenever you give something away, more comes in its place. So if you have been desiring something and you want to receive something, start giving it. If you have been desiring health, start giving health, visualizing health for another friend who perhaps is thinking that they need help or healing. Put yourself in a place of envisioning them healthy and whole, the Christ of them manifesting wholly through the body. And any part of you which has been calling out for healing is going to receive healing tenfold, because as you give, so it is given unto you tenfold.

Now, the importance here is awareness. In other words, as you will envision for another one the wholeness that perhaps you are wanting for yourself, you then want to be in a place of receiving consciously, acknowledging consciously that, "I am receiving the healing that I am giving to another person." Since *there is no separation*, as you give to another, you are giving to yourself, and it has to come, as you see it, back to you.

You can think of ones in your acquaintanceship, and friendship even, who have what are called the million dollars, even the multi-millionaires. You have friends and acquaintances who have many of the golden coins. Now, that one is, in truth, not separate from yourself. In a worldly sense they seem to be separate and they seem to have the power to spend the golden coins in the way that they want to, which they do, and you may feel that you do not have the golden coins, but you do. Begin to take stock, take accounting if you want to call it that, of what you have and what others, as they are seen to be separate from you, have, and step into their sandals.

How would it feel to be Mr. Gates? How would it feel to be able to have so many of the golden coins that you could set up a foundation which would help in various areas of whatever your dream is. Now, does it take a million dollars for you to be able to start to do that? In truth, no. You can start with what you call your five dollars, your ten dollars, your twenty-five. Get others to join in with you. It will grow.

What you have to have is the awareness that you *are* the abundance that has so much to give – and you do – that you can translate it all into a vision, the same as your Mr. Gates took a vision years ago. It was a vision that he loved. It was something that he was very much caught up into and did for the love of it, and the golden coins came.

He did not start out to seek the golden coins; that was not his first mission. He did what he did because he loved doing what he was doing, and the golden coins have come to him. And now he is able to gift the golden coins to many others to help with various projects that they want to do. You can do the same.

So the secret to receiving is to know, first of all, "I already have it." Secondly, to stand in gratitude and to fill up the notebook with listing all of the things you have to be grateful for, and to keep adding to the notebook. And thirdly – I like to teach in three's – to be willing to give; to see what you can give in each day, even in each moment.

You are very rich. Go now and celebrate the richness, and share it with others. As you give, so shall you receive.

Prophecies and the End of a Cycle

Now I would speak with you about something you have been contemplating from time to time. You have wondered, "Why does this Jeshua not speak of certain timelines and certain prophecies? Why does this Jeshua keep it very simple?"

Other entities will speak to you of great federations, and there are those. Others will speak to you of great plans for the future — sometimes dire plans, sometimes more hopeful plans. Others will speak to you of what you have to look out for and what may be coming, and they speak to you of a myriad of things because you are asking, you are inviting, wanting to know all of the dramas, all of these ideas.

It is the same as when you watch your movies, the same as when you turn on your television sets and you tune in to certain programs. You want to know stories. And so there are plenty of entities, plenty of channels that bring you the stories so that you can play with them, so that you can be excited one way or another by what they are telling you.

And you have wondered, "Why is there not prophecy from *this* Jeshua?" Well, I have tried that from time to time, and you have acknowledged that my timing is not your timing. It is because, truly, as we have spoken many times, you are the creators of your reality, the creators of what you experience, and there is always that little bit of improv that you throw in from time to time.

I do not come to give you fanciful stories. I know that you want them, I know that you enjoy them, and I also know that there are many sources that will give them to you. I speak to you from time to time about concepts to show you how they can be clues to what you truly want to remember. But the stories and the concepts are just that. They are stories, they are concepts, and they stay within the mind. The mind plays with them and has great fun.

As you have seen in this reality, you can find one story, one concept, and then you read another book or you go to another website and you will find something opposite it. And you wonder, "Well, is this one true, or is that one true? Which is it? What is going to be happening? I wish somebody would tell me." I have heard you say that.

Truly, no one can tell you except yourself, since the "truth" is based on what you are believing and what you are working towards in your own belief system. I have said to you many times that your so-called future is predicated upon your past — as to what you believe your past has been — and what you usually do is to extend the past into the future.

Now, if you have had a past you believed to be negative, abusive, hard, a struggle—and all of you have known lifetimes like that—then there is a proclivity to look towards the future and say that the future is going to be a struggle. If you have a remembrance of love and of being in harmony, resonance with other ones, then you tend to bring that forward out of your past and project it into the future. But it is all mental, subconscious though it may be, at that point.

What I speak to you is of the heart. That is why I call you the Heart Family, because you *are* of the heart. You play with the mind; you have fun with the mind. The mind will give you all sorts of things to play with. But the mind truly is the servant of the heart, and as you will remember to dwell in the heart, in the place of love, in the place that does not have to understand mentally what love is, but knows it, feels it, and abides in peace, then the mind will set about allowing you to manifest peace and love and harmony and trust.

Go first to the heart. Go to the place of Beholder in love. Then allow the mind to work out what is best for the soul's purpose and the heart's purpose. Play with the mind as much as you want to. You have created it so that you can play with it, the same as you would play with any of the puzzles that you make for yourself or the games that you make. Play with it if you want to, but remember always that everything comes from the place of the heart. That is where your power lies.

Now, within the mental concepts are truths—lower case "t"—and there is a concept that is being widely accepted among those in your grouping of shared belief system that says that the year 2012 is going to be a momentous year, and you should get your ducks in order right now.

You have been wondering, "What more can I do? How can I get my ducks in order when I don't even know where my ducks are? Or how many I might have?" So you do a lot of the mental gymnastics about the year 2012.

Now, there is a thread of truth that runs through this prophecy, because the year 2012 is going to be an advantageous year, but it is not going to be the end of everything. It is going to be part of the process that you are already in, and there will be an extended time from the year 2012 for what you call another five decades after that of a "knowing" that is being already built: the remembrance of your own divinity, of your own power, of where you have come from and *why* you have come.

It has all been in process, and the year 2012 is going to be an advantageous year, because many who are in this grouping of belief system are going to be expecting it, and that which you expect has power, power to manifest.

It is not going to be cataclysmic to the point where it is going to be the end of our holy Mother Earth. It is not going to be the end of this reality. It is going to be an evolutionary process that goes forward and will extend for a good period of time as it grows and evolves upon itself.

You have already set the building blocks in place, and you are going to keep on building. What you will see is a growing awareness within yourself, because you have prayed for this, you have asked for this, you have been preparing for this. There is going to be a growing awareness with the friends and co-workers, and ones who will not even use the same terminology that you use, of their purpose. Many have wondered and are wondering why they are here. They also wonder why they struggle. They wonder, "Am I just here for a short period of time, and is that all there is? Is there just one lifetime?" as is so often put forward in your religious/philosophical threads of thinking: that there is just one lifetime and that there cannot be the reincarnation, the remaking of realities.

So they are questioning, "How do I make the most of this one lifetime?" To introduce to them an idea that perhaps life is ongoing is a bit of an evolutionary leap for them, and yet they are asking to know this. And you are coming into your own power of remembering that you have been here many, many times and that you have choice always whether to return to this reality or any other reality on holy Mother Earth or to go to another constellation or galaxy to adventure in other forms and other ways.

As you remember that you have choice, you begin to feel in the heart the expansion of divinity that is you. After the time period that you call 2012, there is going to be yet a progression of challenges for humankind, but there is also going to be a progression of understanding that the challenges are not so much negative as they are gifts.

It will be a process which will build exponentially upon itself, very much the same as the seed that opens up and comes up through the ground, and then the plant reaches out and will extend a leaf and then another leaf and then another leaf and then a flower and then the fruit.

You are going to be part of it, because you are adding your energy to it. You are going to understand what is going on at a very deep level, and at the same time you are going to be taking part in what seems to be the world level but from a different perspective.

You have manifested this human lifetime so that you could be part of an awakening. There is a cycle, an evolutionary cycle from a place that remembers its divinity, knows that it is creating, into the place where it identifies with whatever is being created and identifies with that creation to the place where it is forgotten, temporarily, who is doing the creating, and then there is the process where you are now: of awakening to realizing, "I am the one who is creating," and then the realization that, "*If* I am creating, I can change whatever I see happening."

And how do you change that? You change it by changing your perception. You have the power at any moment to change your perception of what is going on. No one else can change your perception except you. You have great power, because you *can* change it. No one can take that from you. You are the one who holds the power of perception and of belief, and that is why, when you come to the year of 2012, there is going to be a gathering, a celebration if you will, which you are already planning at a deep level.

The year 2012 is going to be part of the ongoing process of the evolution of awakening. The cycle itself is going to extend past that date.

Every concept that is given to you, every prophecy, every message carries a thread of truth with it. It depends on how you perceive that truth. And I am saying to you, why would you not want to perceive it as good? You have done the suffering already. You have been there, done that. I have been there, done a bit of it, finished with it, completed — as you can be and as you are: complete.

Dream big dreams. Go for it. Allow the dream in the heart to be big, and then allow the mind to figure out how to do it in the world. Do not worry about all of the small details. The mind is going to take care of that. The mind is going to chew on all of the details like a dog chews on a bone. The mind will be very busy as it comes up with the suggestions as to how to do the big dream of the heart.

Take a moment now. Take a deep breath and ask yourself, "What is my dream? If I could have, if I could do, if I could be anything that I want to be or do or have, what would it be? What would I do? Who would I be? How would I be? What is my dream?"

Allow that feeling to stay with you. This evening when you put the head upon the pillow go back to that feeling of, "What do I want in my life? How do I want it to be? How do *I* want to be in my life? What is my greatest desire?" Then live from that space as if it could be true, because it can. You are the one who can make it happen.

The energy of other people that you want to join in with you is going to be there, as well. "I know it. I feel it. I share my dream, my idea with this other person and persons. I share it with myself, all of the aspects of myself. And I feel so uplifted, so excited that I can't wait to talk about it to the other ones." You get together and you are extremely positive about what can be, what you can put together, and you live in a space of possibilities, unlimited possibilities, and it feels so good. And the reason that it feels so good is because it is true.

You are not limited. When you get in the space of excitement and you are talking with another one about what you truly want to do, and they say, "Yes, you can do that. I'll join you. Let's do such and such," you are uplifted out of the world's concerns and struggles, and you live in a divine space. It gives you the feeling that you can do *anything.*

Many of you have felt stuck. You have felt that you had to do such and such because that is what the world expected you to do. You had to earn the golden coins. You had to stay in a certain occupation. You had to go here, go there. Whenever you are thinking about something that you *have* to do and you get the feeling that resonates in the body, it often is right in the solar plexus, and you feel like you could throw it up. Why do you feel, perhaps, nauseous at that point? It is because you truly want, at the soul level, to throw it out and to get rid of it, and sometimes you physically do that.

But when you are living in the space of excitement, of planning unlimited possibilities of what you can do and how you can do them, and you say, "Yes, I can do that," you say "Yes" to your divine power, and everything else has to fall in place, even if separated ego questions your every decision.

Now, you do need to—there is a caveat here—you do need to look at what you might be rebelling against and understand the issues of why maybe you do not feel exactly happy where you are and why you might want to change it all.

Maybe there are issues that need to be looked at and seen with new perspective: to be seen in holiness, to be seen as blessed, so that you do not have to throw it all out, but you can change some of the parts of it. And you can change some of the parts of it without even moving from your chair, because you can change how you look at it. And then sometimes you will make a physical change.

When you live in the place of excitement, you call in all of your angels, your guides, all of the unseen ones who are always around you, but you do not always hear them because you are too focused on what is wrong or what might be wrong or whatever issue might come up. When you are in the place of excitement, you have an opening of energy. You are open to receiving help, assistance from the higher realms. And then what you are planning to do is given more impetus to move forward.

Now, I have said to you many times that you do nothing alone. You may think that you have to make all the decisions yourself. You may think you are doing it all by yourself and that it is a real "heavy" to have to decide something. But truly, you do not do anything alone. Your guides and teachers and angels are always working with you. The wise masters with whom you have walked the face of our holy Mother, the Earth, in physical form in other lifetimes are there to be called upon, as sometimes you have spent the in-between lifetimes being their angel or their guide.

Share your dream, your biggest dream, with others who you know are going to be in a receptive, supportive space. Share with others who will say, "Yes, I believe that for you. I know that to be true. I know you can do that." Share that feeling of power, and know that truly any time you want to call on that power, it is right there within you.

It is what I have spoken of as the Heart, the simplicity of the Heart, not having to worry about all of the details. You allow the mind to play with those, but you abide in the heart, that place of great power, that place of expansion. Then separated ego will run onstage and say, "But master, what about…? How can we do this? They say I can't do this. I'm too old to do this."

Well, you are never too old as long as you draw breath. You are never too old, even if the body has come to a place where it does not move with the flexibility that you used to know, even if the body has to be in a prone position and does not move, even if the body is in one of your wheeled chairs and does not move except as somebody else, perhaps, helps it.

As long as you draw breath you have power to live in that expanded state of excitement about making your dream manifest. So, you see, you have no excuses. As long as you draw breath you are alive, and as long as you are living in this incarnation you can do anything. As long as you draw breath, you are in a place of unlimited possibilities. Let no one tell you what your truth is. Another one can only tell you what their truth is, what their perception is, what their perspective is, but it does not have to be yours, and many times it is not yours. Let no one tell you what your truth has to be, because you are the maker of your truth moment by moment. So you can make your life anything you want it to be, any *how* you want it to be.

You are approaching the end of a cycle of energy where you have gone from knowing the divinity into the most dense of densities, and then you have come to a place where there was a questioning, a clue that perhaps there is more than just what you have termed the Dark Ages. Perhaps there is more than just existence. Perhaps—and you began questioning.

You are now on the upward swing, closing in on what I have called the apogee, the top of the cycle. Many of you will feel the energy expanding and the awareness of divinity and the awakening. You will feel it within the heart and you will know it to be true, even if others would question it.

The end of the cycle is approaching. It is not here just yet, because you have not declared that you want it right now. You want to go through a process. You have agreed to the process of time. So, therefore, you will celebrate the year of 2012 and you will celebrate the year of 2013 and 14 and 15 until you come to a certain place where there is an ending of a cycle for many; not for all, because there are some who yet have a feeling that there is more to experience in the human plane, more of the drama that they want to experience, so they will stay in this reality. But you will not.

You will have finished the cycle, and then you will be looking around to see, "Now what can I play with, where can I go, what can I create?" because the creative One—capital "O"—expresses Itself in myriad forms and places and realities, and the creative One is forever creating and expanding and will forever, beyond time itself, experience and express Itself in new ways. That is what creation is all about. It is about coming up with new ideas. It is about coming up with new creation and sometimes getting drawn into those creations to the place where there is the cycle again of the density and the awakening.

You are very much closing in on the end of the cycle, of *this* cycle. Celebrate, dream the dreams, and share with others the excitement of possibilities.

The Voice of the Brotherhood

I wish to speak to you now about the voice of the Brotherhood. It has been known as the White Brotherhood. It has been known as the Brotherhood of Light. Is there a Brotherhood? Yes, there is. Should we call it a Brotherhood or a Sisterhood? We can call it either one, because it has no gender, truly. But for the patriarchal society throughout generations, it has been known as the Brotherhood. It is truly a coming together of higher understanding.

The higher Selves of you have communion with the Brotherhood. Now, we have spoken many times that you do a most wonderful miracle of focusing upon the self—lower case "s"—the personality, the body of this incarnation. You do a miracle in every moment that says, "This is who I am, this personality, this body, this career; this is who I am," shutting out all of the rest of what you are. It is truly a miracle of creation that you do. And yet you have taught yourself to do it with a precision moment by moment that makes it seem as a continuum, and it is a miracle.

The Council of One is also the Brotherhood or Sisterhood. So perhaps it is of better semantics to speak of it as the Council of One, because you all have a seat at that round table. There is not a higher or lower place; it is a round table, the same as One is in your writing with an O—omega.

The Voice that speaks to you is going to be more and more apparent as time proceeds. You have already decreed that you want to know, "What is life all about?" You have already decreed that you want to know, "How can we bring more harmony, more understanding of myself and others," as you have put it; "how can I bring more and more understanding to my relationships and see the equality of each divine being that is incarnating as a point of Light?"

That is truly Who and What you are: a point of Light. We have talked about how you do the miracle of the coalescence of Light into a denser form to bring about the body. I was here, as you were here, when our holy Mother, the Earth, became a densified being. We, as One, created our holy Mother, the Earth, the earth that so many of the brothers and sisters walk upon in this day and time and take for granted that it is going to be there when they put the foot down. If they were to realize that our holy Mother, the Earth, is Light the same as they are and that it is a miracle every time they put the foot down that there is something underneath the foot that becomes dense in that moment, and may not have been dense the moment before; if they were to realize that, they would stand in awe of the divine energy of being.

Was it solid a moment ago? In truth, no. That boggles the mind a wee bit, because that is not what has been taught to you throughout generations. But you make your own creation moment by moment. And the One that you are, the Voice of the Brotherhood, of the Council of One, the Voice is calling out to you more and more loudly to take a moment to listen; to take a moment to breathe in deeply the inspiration of divine being; the possibility that that which has seemed to be dense—the body, our holy Mother Earth, relationships that seem to be dense—are in truth very malleable, changeable, and that you can change.

You can change yourself and you can change what is happening around you. It is powerful when you begin to remember What you are; not just who you are, because that brings it back to feeling that you are a certain personage. But when you begin to remember What you are, the extension of the one Creator, the one creative Isness, Thought Itself going forward, creating moment by moment the very chair that you sit on, creating moment by moment the very vehicle that you drive, creating moment by moment the reality that you say you live in, and when you stop and you listen for the Voice, it changes everything around you.

And so you begin to live from a space of Light, Lightheartedness. You begin to live from a place that says, "This is a reality. Whatever befalls me in a day, as far as experiences, that is part of reality, but it is not all of reality, and I can understand it in a greater context as I listen for the voice of my higher Self, the voice that is not attached to the body or to this reality."

Now, the habitual way of looking at things is to make instant judgment, and that has served you very well for generations and eons of time, because it has allowed you to defend, to keep in the same state of beingness that which you thought was important—the body, the dwelling place, the loved ones.

But you have also seen that you are repeating patterns, and with the realization that you are repeating a pattern—you even have a saying in this world that history repeats itself—when you have realized that there is a repeating pattern, there is the moment of awakening. That is the moment when you begin to ask, "What more is going on here?" That is the moment when you listen for the Voice of the Brotherhood.

Now, we are all equal masters. That is very, very difficult to accept, as you see yourself just to be human. You have not been taught by your religious/philosophical authorities that we are equal. All of the religious/philosophical orders have had a great teacher that they have listened to in the beginning, caught some of the great ideas and gained enlightenment, and then as time went on, the teacher has been elevated to a pedestal way above any of the common people.

But the Truth is that we are all equal masters, all extensions of Life in various forms and understandings.

You are going to want to know the Voice of the Brotherhood that is removed enough into the place of

Beholder that we have spoken of many times, into the place of Beholder where the whole picture can be seen, the holy picture—w-h-o-l-e / h-o-l-y—the whole tapestry of what is going on; not just one or two or three threads of the tapestry, but to be able to catch hold of the whole picture and to see which thread you are, and to see how you weave with the other threads to make the most wonderful evolution of human consciousness to the place of remembrance of divinity.

That is what you are working towards: the place of remembrance of the Consciousness of divinity which allows you to be the extension and the expression of divinity even in a reality that does not believe that there could be divine intervention.

Divine intervention? That is you. Every time you choose to listen to the Voice; every time you choose to come up higher in your understanding of Who and What you are and Who and What the other brothers and sisters are, you have done divine intervention. You have allowed the power of the master that you are to step down the vibration enough to make the density of a body, to live within a reality that yet says that it is dense. But at any moment you are able to do the divine intervention of saying, "Hey, I am the master that is creating moment by moment. I am creating this body, this experience, this reality."

And in that moment everything has to change. In that moment of divine realization of What you are—the same as I am, the Christ—that is divine intervention at its highest level. The Christ of you walks this Earth and can see it once again in its beauty, in its original beauty as the Light Being that She is.

Allow yourself to be the divine intervention that cleans up holy Mother Earth by your thoughts and by your actions. Allow yourself to live in joy and to appreciate the Light Being that we brought into manifest form cooperatively as holy Mother Earth. Recognize her Voice calling to you.

It is the simple life of trust, listening to the Voice which allows you to know that you are not confined to this reality. As you will allow yourself to listen to the still, small Voice, the Voice of the Brotherhood, the Voice of the Council of One, the Voice of the master that you are, you will take a deep breath and you will allow; judge not.

Judge not, lest ye be judged, because in that moment you are judged by your own judgment, standing in the middle of the hayfield of judgment. Allow yourself to listen to the Voice of the master that you are, to see everything from a place of Light. Allow even the molecules of whatever seems to be dense to expand so that you see the light in between every molecule, the light that is in between every word that is spoken, every thought that is thought, every choice that is made. Allow yourself to focus on the Light. And that, beloved one, will bring you Home. Come Home unto me.

The New Decade

Beloved friend, peace be with you. I am the one known as Joseph, Earthly father to the one you have known as Jeshua, and beloved husband of the one you now call Mother Mary.

I had my own life, my own identity as Joseph, and I lived that lifetime happily in the Essene community. After releasing the body in that lifetime, there were other lifetimes when I collected much wisdom, the same as you are doing now, and I brought the wisdom once again into an incarnation which you now have called St. Germain.

It is from the vantage point as St. Germain that I would speak with you now, for there is a message from the Council of One that has been given to me to pass along to you. You have heard of the Council of One. It is truly the council of all of the higher souls, the souls that have come into awakening.

Even though you have focus upon your present personality and lifetime, you are part of the Council of One, for in truth there is no separation. We are all One. We are All of the divine one Mind. As you have heard it said, you are the expression of the one creative Principle come forth into various realities to try out different scripts, to try out how it would be to create, and vast and myriad have the creations been and will continue to be, even outside of what you see now this reality to be, even outside of what you would define as a physical reality.

The realities will continue, and that is why the Council of One has asked me to speak with you now as you embark upon a new decade. You have come through the experience of moving into a new millennium where there were many prophecies, including many negative prophecies, because this reality believes in duality, where there can be good and the opposite of good. Some of the prophecies were quite dire.

Well, you came into this new millennium and guess what? The computers still worked, the washing machines still worked, the telephones still worked, and you kept waiting for a few months into the new millennium for disaster, perhaps, to come from the skies, forgetting that you are the creative ones who bring forth everything, and you are the ones who then judge whatever comes forth, whether it be good or medium or not so good.

You also came into a new century, and you wondered as you moved into the new millennium and embarked upon the new century, "What is this century going to bring?" You looked back to the previous century and you saw an evolution of awareness that was quite tumultuous, quite representative of the belief in duality, for there were the world wars, as they were called, where many countries were engaged on one side *and* on the other side, believing in separation and believing that new technology would solve everything.

But you also looked back at previous centuries and there was hope and optimism that truly you could be moving into another Golden Age. Now, you have known some five centuries or so ago an Age of Enlightenment, an age when there was much of evolutionary thought that went beyond the dark, the so-called Dark Ages.

Then there was a balancing in this reality where if you have something on one hand, pretty soon you are going to have something on the other hand to balance it out, so that you have come through some centuries since the Age of Enlightenment to a place where the enlightenment and the darkness have interchanged with each other at various times.

So the first decade of the new century of the new millennium has been a working out, a review, if you will, of what has been in the past centuries.

You are now moving into the next decade of this new century and new millennium, and it is going to be one of excitement for you. There is going to be a winding down of some of the conflicts that you have seen going on, because the younger generations are going to be tired. Even though the habitual generational thinking has been all that they have known and all that they have been taught, they are going to begin to ask, "Is there not another way?"

In the next decade you will be interacting with ones that you see face to face and you are going to be interacting with other ones that are as a potential face to face, ones you have known in other lifetimes and constellations, who have agreed to meet up with you once again at a specified time within this reality. Furthermore, you will be interacting with ones that are within the mind and within the memory.

Sometimes you feel a presence around you that perhaps you can identify as a friend who has released the body or a loved one who has released the body or an ascended master whom you have read about, and you feel, "This one cannot be here with me." But this one is. Where else would they go? They are within your field of energy as you are within their field of energy. This awareness is going to be the most important part of the new decade: knowing the energy that you are and the energy of all ones, whether they are in physicality or in mind, Intelligence—capital "I".

Awareness of Energy is going to be the most pivotal point of the next decade. You are going to feel and experience the world in a different way, and others are going to know it because of how you go in your life, knowing that you are truly not the body, you are not the personality, you are the energy of an ascended master radiating forth the Intelligence.

You are all ascended masters who have agreed one more time that you will descend into this reality that is not your home, that is not the place where you want to abide forever, but you have agreed that you will bring your energy and your Light and your laughter into this reality that believes itself so seriously to have to judge, to have to struggle.

This next decade is going to be a movement into knowing non-separation. You are going to see separation still with some worldly affairs. You are still going to see separation of bodies. But you are also going to understand that the bodies are not solid. They are forever changing as your energy patterns change.

You have the technology for reading the auras already, for having the photographs that show the change in the auric pattern as you have different emotions or as you think different thoughts. The photographs are proof for you, because this reality yet wants to see the proof out there before the understanding and truth is then accepted within.

The new decade is going to fine-tune a knowing, the same knowing that you feel when you hug another one and you are in love with that other one, where you know yourself to be One with that other one—just for an instant, perhaps, or longer. When you are in that embrace, truly what you have done is to bring the energy fields together even closer, into a place where you can feel—if you tune in to it—the vibrational level of love.

This decade is going to see a change in how you view yourself, how you view others, and how you view the world situation. You are not going to deny the Earthly conditions. If you are in a position where your help is needed, you will give the physical help, you will give the golden coins if that is what is needed, you will help ones as your guidance tells you to do.

In this next decade, because you are going to understand the great ball of energy that you are—and I do not mean that you are overweight—you are going to feel yourself totally, happily alive, and you are going to be very intuitive as to others' energy, where they feel themselves to be.

Now, this is already happening, but it is going to increase. As this awareness increases, you are going to also know how to keep your balance, to keep your feeling of joy in the face of others who are finishing or completing their dramas. You will not be disruptive to their dramas, but you will keep your own balance within yourself.

Your planet, this most beautiful planet that we have brought forth, is changing. You have noticed some of the climate changes. You have noticed the intensity of some of the storms and the change in weather patterns. You have either been experiencing it where your dwelling place is or where the loved ones and friends are dwelling.

There has been an intensity of energy patterns swirling around this planet. Those patterns come from the collective consciousness. Where else could they come from if all is One? They also come from your directive; in other words, you can direct a storm away from wherever you are if you know that you can do this, and you can.

For other ones, they may decree that they want to know the adrenaline rush of a storm. If you want to do that, there is no judgment. It is an experience. But if you do not want to experience the intensity of a storm—call it a tornado, a thunderstorm, even a snowstorm—if you do not want the hurricane coming to your dwelling place, you can direct it out to sea, up into the upper atmosphere. You can direct it, because it is connected to your energy. All is One.

The intensity of the storms that you see happening now and the swirling of the climate change that is happening is coming from the collective consciousness that is sometimes throwing a temper tantrum, and so you see the out-picturing of that energy. It may be coming from confusion within the collective consciousness and so it is out-pictured, again, as a clearing, as a storm that will come through and will clear the energy.

Now, there *are* climate changes that are happening. There *is* global warming, and it *is* due to humankind. Yes, you are the reason for the global warming, but that is not said in judgment as a negative thing. It is said to allow you to understand how powerful you are, how you bring forth changes, how you have asked for evolutionary changes in what grows upon this planet, what form of the animal life is going to be upon the planet. For truly, as one species may seem to leave the planet, another species is born. There is never a vacuum. There is always a change which is happening.

So you can take responsibility for the global warming. The global warming comes because you are stepping up your vibratory rate as the collective. And, again, there is no judgment in it. It is an experience.

Nothing is ever lost. The form may change. The species may change, and things may look different, feel different. Your historians have told you of the ice ages, and you have evidence of the glaciers and the glacial rubbish, the rocks that have been left behind by the glaciers of other times. So this is not something that you are bringing about as disaster. It is part of what you have decreed that you will know as change, because the collective consciousness of the human is one that desires to know change.

If truth be told, and I *will* tell it, all of creative Intelligence wants to know change. You *are* the extension of the one creative Principle; therefore, you are going to keep on creating. There is nothing wrong with change. Flow with it. Welcome it. Look for new species of flowers, trees, plants, animals, even humankind. Know you that in what you would call prehistory the human form—you do know this, because some of your scientists have taught you this, although there are ones who do not believe in evolution, as it is called—you had heavy fur covering on the body. You still have some of that left. Some of the men, you still have some of the heavy fur covering around the chin.

So in this next most wonderful decade that you are just now walking into, there is going to continue to be an evolution of humankind – not especially in the appearance but in recognizing and acknowledging that which you are in energy. Because truly, no matter how much makeup the woman or man puts on, how much of the raiment you change and put on, the energy that you are is going to be obvious. Everyone will feel and know if it is a loving energy or if it is a confused energy or an angry energy, and there will be no hiding it.

The awareness is going to be accentuated in your next decade, because ones are going to feel—especially those of you who are already the sensitives—are going to be feeling energy within themselves, and you will be able to catch yourself as you begin to perhaps close down, or as you perhaps feel a bit of the rising of the volcano of energy.

Begin to build up a self esteem, and begin to feel then the expansion of your energy, where you feel at peace with yourself and you feel at peace with others, because truly no one can touch your peace. You are the only one who can affect your peace, and that is only temporary.

More and more you are going to come truly alive as the energy that you are, as the walking, moving, loving, living Energy that you are.

Your energy truly reaches the farthest galaxies, because there is no separation in Mind—capital "M". There is no separation. It is all creative Principle.

So be it.

— *Joseph/St. Germain*

The Measure of Mastery

Beloved one, every lifetime you have left a mark upon our holy Mother Earth—sometimes a physical mark, but I mean more the spiritual mark. You have made impact, and you have left a measure of your energy. It is there when you go back and you visit what would be a foreign land or a new place, and you find something that feels familiar. It is because you have left your energy in those places.

Everywhere you walk you leave an imprint. You even have in your world now a focusing upon what is called the carbon footprint and how big your footprint is in the global focus of energy. Everywhere you have gone in this lifetime and other lifetimes you have made impact of one sort or another.

You have chosen some great challenges and some smaller challenges in order to live your divine being. It was the same for me: would I travel to far lands to study with the great masters of that time, would I teach the multitudes or just the few, would I experience the crucifixion and arise up in the resurrection to continue that lifetime? These were some of the choices I looked at in that lifetime.

Take yourself back…in this moment, allow yourself the deep breath, and allow yourself to go back to the being that you have been in the Atlantean time when you were the creator bringing forth new creative inventions, when you were working with crystals, and when you were finding what crystals could do as you were knowing Oneness with the energy of a crystal.

Allow yourself to feel how you felt and to see the goal that you had in that lifetime as to how you wanted to use the energy of the crystals. Some of you in a particular lifetime saw the energy of the crystal to convey to you personal power. Others of you saw the healing energy of the crystal and how it could be used for healing.

In the last couple of moments you have traveled, as your historians measure time, back many, many eons of time to a realization, a reality that is true; it is legendary according to some of your history books, if it is mentioned at all, but it is true. It is a true reality that you have lived. You have been there.

You have also walked the path of peace with nature in Lemuria. Feel you that peace and know that that peace of nature can be found yet. There are some of your trees which have been growing for centuries of time; allow yourself to sit with them in the mind, and sometimes with the physical body, and to ask of them what they have seen and what they would advise for the future.

Everything is open to you. Everything. There is nothing that is held away from you. There is nothing that would be denied. It cannot be denied the holy creative Child that you are. That is why I encourage you to go for it, to live your dream, to ask of yourself what is your dream? What do you want to see happening in your own life? What do you want to see happening with the grouping of friends? What do you want to see upon the face of our holy Mother, the Earth?

You are a great master. You have chosen to be in this reality at this time, just as you have chosen many other times when there would be a turning of an age, a time of awakening. You have said, "I want to be there for the quickening of the energy. I want to be there to add my energy to it."

You are a courageous master. You have come from the place of the heart. That is what the root of the word courageous comes from—*coeur*—the heart. You come from the heart to serve the Light, to serve the awakening one more time.

The measure of a master, and the measure of mastery itself, is very simple. The measure of mastery is in the time that it takes you to be in the place of turmoil, to understand the place of confusion, and then to come to peace. Sometimes it may take you a decade or longer. They call it a certain stage of life. You may have to live through a certain stage of life. Other times it may take you a couple of weeks. Other times it may take you only a deep breath, and then you come to that place of peace that says, "Whatever happens is good, because it serves the atonement. Whatever happens, I add my energy of knowing the blessedness of it, and therefore it *is* good."

So if you want to know the measure of how you as a master are coming along with this journey, if you want the progress report, you can do this for yourself easily. When you get into that place where you do not know what to do, or you feel that everything seems to be at sixes and sevens and nothing is working together, allow yourself the deep breath and come to the place of peace. If it does not happen right away, that is okay. Take another deep breath and ask for peace. If it takes you an hour, a day, a fortnight, even a year to be at peace with something, that is okay. That is the measure of mastery.

If you would cast your mind back to a decade ago when you were in a certain situation and there was perhaps an issue that was very close to your heart and it hurt, now you look at it and you see it differently. You can see the blessing that has been in it and the goodness in it, even though at the time, a decade ago, it might have been very painful.

The measure of mastery can happen with the deep breath in an instant, or it may take longer, and that is okay. There is no judgment, because truly there is no time. In this reality there seems to be time, but in truth, it does not matter if it takes you lifetimes before you have lived a certain situation over and over and over and then finally come to a place where you have said, "It really doesn't matter. It really doesn't affect me at all, what 'they' choose to do."

But sometimes in a lifetime it seems very important what "they" have chosen to do, and you can feel very hurt by what they have chosen to do. But then you can come to a place where you say, "That touches me not. It is *their* choice.

It is what *they* see to be important that they need to do," and you can let it go.

The measure of a master can be measured by how long or short a time it takes you to come to that place of peace. It can be done, as I said, with the deep breath. It can be done with the candle. If you are wanting to work with something tangible, light a candle and look into the flame, the energy of the candle, and know yourself to be that light, for truly, you are the one creating the light of the candle. In truth, that candle does not exist except as you have brought it forth in your consciousness.

Now, the world does not say that to you. The world says that if you touch the flame, you are going to feel it. But that is the teaching of the world, and you can go beyond that. You have seen ones snuff out the candle flame with their fingers, and you wonder, "How can they do that? That's fire. How can they snuff out that flame with their fingers?" You have thought, "If I did that, it would be too hot."

But if you are in a certain state of mind and you reach out and you squeeze the flame, you can extinguish it with no harm to the fingers. It is the state of mind, the consciousness that makes the difference. However, I would suggest that as you develop trust in knowing the shift in consciousness, for the first few times you snuff the candle flame, you wet your fingers first. (Smile) It is the state of mind, it is the consciousness that determines what you see your life to be and how you see it to be.

Some of you have wondered, "Why am I here? I enjoy my life, I enjoy traveling, I enjoy my friends, I enjoy the books that I read, but why am I here? Surely there has to be a reason more than that." It is to *be* the Light that lifts up the world. It is to be the master in realization and to know that every issue that comes to you, you have invited.

Now, sometimes separated ego does not want to hear that. "I invited this mess? I invited this relationship? I invited all of this abuse? I have invited the illness? I have invited the economic downturn?" Yes, you have, in order to know your divine power, in order to know the divine power of choice to live in a different space.

That is what I have called the measure of mastery, to be able to choose to live in the space of divine love, a space that knows that no matter what the world is doing, no matter what the body seems to be doing, no matter what anyone else is doing, "I am living the I Am Intelligence. I Am Love. I am okay." Start with that one. You can understand that one, the human self. "I am okay." And you are. You are truly more than okay, but sometimes separated ego does not want to go any further than that, so you can start with, "I am okay…I think." And you are.

Allow yourself in every day to celebrate your Self. And by that, I mean to look back over the challenges, the experiences of this lifetime and to see where you have come. See where you were a decade ago. Separated ego may say, "Well, a decade ago I was younger. I was prettier; I was more handsome. I had more golden coins. I had more of the worldly accolades…." Maybe yes, maybe no.

But as you will assess the measure of mastery, you will realize that now you can come to the place of peace much more quickly than you did previously. You can come to the place where you are okay with whatever anyone else chooses. You are okay with whatever the body brings to you. You are okay with every issue, because you know that you are more than any issue.

Some of the issues feel like big stumbling blocks. You lose a loved one and they do not send you a post card, and it feels big. But the master of you—and you *are* a master—comes to know that that experience was not a downer. It was not a minus sign, but a plus, and you look at all of the treasure that came from whatever issue you have dealt with or are dealing with. You look at all of the expansion of experience that it brings to you instead of looking at all that you have lost, because truly you never lose anything anyway.

103

You look at all of the positive things that have come out of that experience, all of the treasures that you have stored away in the treasure chest, and only you know those treasures. You can open that treasure chest and you can take out each jewel and look at it and say, "This is the jewel that came from when my parents left. This is the jewel that came when my mate left. At the time I thought it was a piece of coal, an old stone, an old rock. I would have thrown it away, but something told me to put it in the treasure chest. Now I see that there are sparkles on it, and it looks different to me."

That is the measure of the master: to be able to see the good very quickly in everything that you experience. As you travel the journey of life, there are many opportunities to judge; to judge self: that is the first one. You have been taught, even subconsciously, by the parents and the peers that you were not quite good enough. Maybe you did not make the cheerleading squad. Maybe you did not make the first string of the football team. Maybe you were not the best orator. Maybe you did not get the highest grades, etc.

The peers would tell you whether you were good enough or not good enough, and the parents—even the most well-meaning parents—would encourage you to do better. And you thought, "Well, if they are saying that I should do better, that means that I'm not there yet, I'm not perfect yet, so I must be imperfect."

Your heavenly Father/Mother sees you as perfect, because you have to be. You are the extension of that creative Principle. It is neutral. There is no good or bad, less or more. It Is, and there is no judgment in it.

Allow yourself to know that you are the master come once again into this experience to let your Light shine, to be joyful in the face of sorrow, to be comforting to another one and to lift them up with hope.

Know that always I am here for you. If there is no one else who will listen to you, I will listen to you. Always I hear you when you call. Call upon me.

Let Not Your Heart Be Troubled

Beloved one, it is a most wonderful time that you are living in now, because everything is changing. You have prayed for change. You have prayed for heaven on Earth, and in order to have heaven, you have to make room for the new. Until now—in recorded history and even some of the pre-history—this reality has not been heaven. It has been more of an experience in duality.

So I say unto you, it is a most blessed time, even though separated ego is going to be screaming at you from time to time that this does not feel good. But that is the job of separated ego: to point out to you when you have come into the place of believing yourself to be separate, believing yourself to be vulnerable, believing yourself to be powerless.

In those moments there are practical things that you can do to bring yourself back to the place of Oneness, beginning with imagining yourself to be One with anyone or any part of nature. It is the Truth of your being, but you can start with imagining.

Imagine yourself to be the dandelion—most wonderful name, dandy lion. How would it feel to be the dandelion? It is the most beautiful sunshine that is blooming and it is called a weed; truly it is a flower. Because it grows so profusely, you have termed it a weed and you try to get rid of it. But it has the last laugh, because it has so many little seedlings which it puts up into the air that you never get rid of it. It comes back.

Allow yourself to play with, "How would it feel to be a dandelion and to know my power: that truly others who walk on the two feet and think that they have control over their most wonderful manicured lawns cannot have power over me, because I am going to let the wind take my seedlings everywhere." A dandelion does not ever feel that it can be vanquished. It cannot.

When I studied in what is now known as Britain with the Druid masters, there were techniques that they shared with me to allow me to remember once again my divine Oneness, to truly know it at a very deep level within me, not just the intellectual, which I had known from the Essene school in copying the written scrolls of ancient wisdom; I knew much of the mystical teachings. But when I went to study with the Druids, it was a different approach.

They spoke to me of the four elements: earth, wind, fire, and water. Now, you have that repeated with your First Nation, the Native American culture in this geographical part of the world. They also have a common heritage with the Druids from before there was a separation. So if you are looking to know connection with Self—capital "S"—allow yourself to play with the earth, the soil. Go out and dig in the soil and get it right under the fingernails.

Put the hand into the soil and allow yourself to feel that you are growing as a plant does. Stay there long enough to feel yourself grounded, rooted in the soil with both hands. Allow yourself to become One in your knowing with the earth, with Mother Earth as the soil.

Then on another level allow yourself to know Oneness with Mother Earth as the Light Being which she is, because as you play in the soil, there is going to come to you a radiance, a vibratory feeling as you allow the hand to stay there. Bring your awareness to the soil.

Wind. Another technique which the Druids practiced whenever they felt the world was too much with them was to find a place where the wind was blowing, preferably a strong wind, and allow it to cleanse them, to blow off all of the feathers of problems, right down to the Self, to the holy Self.

If it is a still day and there is not much wind blowing, I know that many of you, if not all, have what is called the electrical device known as the fan. So you can plug in the fan, even if it is wintertime, and stand in front of it and allow it to blow all of those problems away from you.

Now, when I studied with the Druids, there was not a problem of finding wind, because we were on the seacoast and there was always a wind blowing in from the sea. But if you have a problem finding a good wind blowing and you need a strong one, turn on the electrical fan and put it on "high", and stand in front of it until you feel that you have been cleansed of all of the old issues, all of the old feathers. And while you are doing that, remember to breathe. Breathe of the wind, of the air, especially if you are out on the beach, especially if you are out in nature. But you can do it indoors with the fan, as well. Remember to take the deep breath.

Fire. A most powerful cleansing agent. I would suggest that you start with a small bit of fire. Do not go out immediately and set fire to your dwelling place and say, "Oh, I needed a big bonfire." Allow yourself to start with the candle and the candle flame. Gaze into the flame. Feel yourself totally immersed in that light to the point where you do not see anything else but the flame of the candle. Know yourself to be One with the candle flame, the little flickering flame which has the potential of great power.

Sometimes you feel like a little flickering flame, not sure you can keep on burning. But your potential is great, and once you catch fire, there is very little that can stop you. Allow yourself to gaze into the flame of the candle and feel yourself to be One. For a moment or so, forget all that has been bothering you. Know yourself to be that light, for you are creating that light even as you see it. That is how powerful you are.

Water. Now, you know that the body is vibratory light brought into a density that seems to be separate from other bodies. It is also made up of over ninety percent water. Allow yourself to take a container of water, a glass or a cup, and hold it in your hand and focus on the vibration. You will feel a vibration. You may feel that you are imagining it, but it is truly your vibration and the water's vibration in synchronicity with each other. Allow yourself the focus that says, "I am free. I am perfect. I am loved. I am so loved that I am Love itself." Put that feeling into the water and the water will respond. It will accept your thoughts. And then allow yourself to drink from it many times during the day.

You do not have to drink gallons of water. Even what has been said to you, that you have to have eight glasses of water in a day, is not true. It is very good for the trips to the little room, but in truth, allow yourself to drink the amount that feels natural to you. There is no set amount, because bodies are different. Different bodies will ask of you different amounts of water. So the eight glasses of water may be right for the person who first suggested it; maybe they were quite large and there needed to be a good bit of the water going through them. Perhaps a smaller size body does not need as much. Drink what is comfortable for you.

Now, another way to experience Oneness with water is to take the shower or bath. If you do a bath, I suggest that you slide down into the bath to the place where you have just the nose above, and then take a deep breath and go all the way under. Pretend to be the little puppy dog that comes up out of the water and shakes. Know you how freeing that feels?

Allow yourself to go down under the water and come back up again and shake it all off. And when you are shaking it all off, know that everything that you have been worried about up to that point has gone flying off of you, out of your focus, away. And if it does not feel complete, do it again and again and again. You can do the same thing when you are under your shower. Stand under the flowing water that is coming down on the head, and then step back for a moment and shake it all off. Have great fun.

You can also allow yourself to find water that is out in nature. If you do not swim well, you put on what are called the little floating wings that will support you so that you do not go straight to the bottom and have to be fished out. You wear the water wings.

Allow yourself to walk into the water, to jump into the water, to be submerged in the water in nature if you have it accessible to you. The Druids knew how to do that because they were on the seacoast, and they knew the power of water to cleanse both body and mind.

So now you have some of the tools that the Druids shared with me. In times when you feel that everything is going wrong, allow yourself to use some of these tools that we have spoken of to come to a place of peace for a moment or longer.

Sometimes you will reach that place of peace and then it slips away. Go back to it. That is the discipline. Go back to it. It takes practice. It takes discipline. But no one can take the reward from you.

When you reach the place of peace, there is no one who can take that from you. When you have the discipline to come back to that place of peace again—and I know there are times when the heart is hurting and the ego is screaming that, "They should not have given me the pink slip. I worked for this company twenty years, and I worked night and day, and there were times when I put in overtime and I wasn't even paid for it, and I even went home and I didn't have my mind on the family, because I was working on this project, and they gave me this pink slip. Why? I didn't deserve that. There were other ones who came along after me who were with the company less time, and they didn't get a pink slip. Why me?"—bring yourself back to the place of peace. Use one of the tools that we have spoken of; whatever works for you, whatever draws you to the place where you find peace.

And when you reach that place, no one and no thing can disturb you. When you reach that place, there is great joy, because you know that never again will you be vulnerable to anyone, to anything that they do or say or think. It is a place of great power, a place of great peace.

Count everything as a blessing, even if it does not look like it, and oftentimes in the beginning, the pink slip does not look like a blessing. The lover who says, "I don't love you any more," does not look like a blessing. The financial challenges, where you have lost all of the savings, the retirement money, does not look like a blessing. And yet throughout all of the challenges that come to you is the opportunity for freedom, the opportunity to grow in another way and to come to the place that knows, truly knows the power and the peace which the world cannot disturb or take away from you.

Then you abide in the place of the Christ.

Origin and Future of Planet Earth

I would speak with you now of the origin and history of your planet, our holy Mother, the Earth, and how the planets came to be. In the beginning, before ever there was even the thought of time, there was Thought. There was an awareness, a presence, if you will, of creative Isness, extending Itself. And there was thought to bring forth expression of the creative Energy, for energy cannot be contained. The energy of the Isness of you cannot and never will be contained within any sphere of any reality — small "r." The Reality — capital "R" — of you is ever expanding. The one Mind is ever expanding, ever expressing and experiencing.

There was thought to bring forth Light and from that Light to bring forth form out of Light, to coalesce Light into form. And from that one instant outside of time, because it was not thought to have time at that point, there was form brought together as the energy, brought together into form which coalesced into what you now still can see in your heavens as various constellations, the galaxies and various bodies of energy in which you lived, in which you knew your existence, in which you knew you were the energy of Thought.

Now, I speak here as it would be in linear fashion of a past time, and yet there was not thought of time yet at that point. There was only thought of creation. Time, the understanding of time, came later. So even as your scientists now will measure the light from the galaxies that are far away, it is measured in light years, and it is measured in linear time.

But, in truth, what you brought forth is even older than what your scientists are telling you now, or *can* tell you now, because your scientists are yet circumscribed by the concept of the sphere of time. They do very well with it, taking you to the very edge of the sphere of time, but to go beyond that, it is a bit like your explorers who at first thought that the Earth was flat, and that if you went beyond a certain point on the horizon, you would fall off.

Your scientists are yet working with concepts within the understanding of time, and yet they are making breakthroughs to understand that thought and the energy of thought does not need to and, in truth, cannot be contained even within time. So in what you would see to be eons and eons of time ago, you lived and moved and had your being in the farthest galaxies of the universe. You knew yourself to be creative; you knew yourself to be the flow of thought and of energy. As you experienced various forms of stellar bodies, you knew yourself to be even the sun. You *were* the activity and the energy, and still are, of the sun and of each star.

You knew yourself to be the extension of Energy that went beyond that sun or that star; very expansive, no limitations. You played with that for what you now understand to be eons of time until there was a thought, "Let us see what else we can create." And then there were more of the galaxies created within the vast universe, which is still expanding.

You played on your way to this solar system; you played in other star constellations–the Pleiades, Sirius, Arcturus and others as well–many different ones where you have known the experience and expression of holy Isness, creative Isness, places where you brought forth great civilizations as you would now, in a broad term, look at civilizations.

And you brought forth technology, as you would have, again, the broad understanding of technology. It was not exactly what you have now. You brought forth the spaceships to travel, and not the slow ones that you understand now: you would go with the speed of thought, faster than the speed of light.

You are the explorers. You are the ones who want to know the farthest frontiers. And when you get to whatever would seem to be a frontier, well, it is as the idea of the Earth being flat, so that you might fall off at the edge of the horizon. You find that when you get to the horizon, there is another horizon beyond, etc. So the explorers that you are, you keep creating. Why? For the sheer joy of it; because you *want* to create. You want to experience and express the divinity of you. You want to know the power of your divinity—not the power of the world; you have played with that many times—but the power that is now coming into even the collective consciousness: the power of divinity, the power of thought, the power of going beyond what ones have said the box has to be.

So now when you go out and you look into your heavens, you see the light of stars and constellations where, in truth, you did and are having expression, even now. For as your scientists will tell you about the light years that it takes for the light to come from a certain other solar system or another constellation, know you that you were standing upon some of the energy bodies even in *that* time. And now you are looking at yourself standing here looking back at the self. It is a thought that allows the mind to expand a bit.

So as you wanted to, and as is your nature to be expansive, you kept expanding the universe itself. In working with the creative energy, there are times when you wanted to bring forth something new, and you did what is known as the involution of energy, the black holes they are called, where you would bring in a lot of the energy into quite dense form to then create anew, because it is part of what you want to prove to yourself, the one Mind, how expansive, how creative you can be.

You have played with the various constellations and on the planets of the various constellations. You have played within *this* solar system on other planetary bodies. At first you began with being the sun, the energy of the star, being within the sun itself, knowing the consciousness of the energy of the star. From that there was expansion to create other bodies of form upon which you could play, making what you call now the planets, the different ones that encircle the sun, and the solar energy, which is still you. You are still within your sun, your star. But you are also, vast creative Being that you are, having a focus of attention on *this* lifetime where you walk upon the surface of *this* planet.

Now, when this planet was first formed, you lived within this planet; you were within it, it was within you, and you lived within it as consciousness. Then there was thought to see, "What else could there be?" And ones would characterize this as then coming up to the surface. It was not so much that you physically came up to the surface as it was the consciousness expanded to take in all that you were creating. And the planet, as you have understood it, has undergone many changes.

You have played on the other planets of this solar system as well, for you are not content, wanderer that you are, to play on just one planet. We have spoken in other times of the planet Maldek and how you played out a most wonderful civilization and drama with advanced technology, to the place where there was the explosion of the planet itself into what you have now as the asteroid belt, the pieces of drifting physical forms of energy.

Some of the energy from the planet Maldek went to another planet known as Jupiter and became part of the mass of Jupiter; also, it became some of the moons of Jupiter. The physical energy also went to become some of the rings of Saturn and also some of the mass of Saturn. Those two planets, especially, are much larger. That is because they absorbed some of the energy from Maldek.

The planet you call Mars is now being the object of investigation as to whether or not there was ever life on Mars. Of course, there was. Were you there? Yes, you were there.

You have in your history an occurrence which has been known as the ice age, of which there have been many, where there was much of ice upon the Earth. At the time of the explosion of Maldek the rippling effect of that energy evaporated most of the surface water on Mars and sent it outward. There is still water on Mars, but much of the water on the surface came to Earth in the extended heat of the explosion, melting some of the ice on Earth and adding to the amount of water on the Earth. Our holy Mother, the Earth, did not always have as much water as She does now. Land masses changed, here and on Mars.

As you have known lifetimes upon other planets of other solar systems in other constellations, you have come to this planet as starseeds. Even from Maldek and Mars you have brought with you remembrances and cultural influences. We have spoken previously that, as starseeds, you are in the process of blending many cultural beliefs and systems of belief into a harmonious whole: that which I have called the atonement, the awakening as One.

Many of you are going to return to some of the other constellations where you feel a call. You will spend what is seen now in your linear terms to be several more lifetimes, perhaps, on this planet, because you have agreed that you will bring your Light *here*, and that you will bring the expanded understanding of how this planet came to be and what it is for, but in what you see to be, again linear time, in the future, many of you are going to feel a call to return through the stargates.

Now, we have spoken of the stargates previously, how they have been closed and how they are now opening. They were closed at the time of the destruction of Maldek, because it was felt by the Council of One that the collective consciousness in this solar system was too focused upon its very small self and how the divine power of creativity could be used in a way that was not beneficial or harmonious with the other constellations, so that the stargates were temporarily closed to communication until this collective consciousness matured a bit.

You are now coming to a place where the stargates are opening, where there can be and is communication with other constellations, with other intelligences from other constellations, and other forms of life. Your astro-scientists have recently identified a planet in the constellation Leo which does sustain life. There is now an expansion that the collective consciousness has agreed to experience. So the stargates are opening, and with the opening is coming right now a trickle—but it will become a flood later on—of information, remembrance of where you have been and how you have been.

This planet, our holy Mother Earth, will continue to be for what you see to be a long, long time, because *she* has volunteered to be part of the divine energy, to serve as a place where ones can play in what I have likened unto the sandbox, where ones can play in the sandbox harmoniously with each other—or not.

There is always choice. But there will come a time when the purpose of the planet will be fulfilled, when the thought energy will be withdrawn from it, and it will be allowed to become part of the light of the whole of the cosmos, free-flowing as it was before it was formed. Now, it is not something that you have to sit here in this day and time and contemplate and wonder, "When is this going to happen; am I going to be here; do I need to dig my shelter somewhere in the ground, and if I do, have I found a sacred spot?"

As I have said, many of you will not be here at that time, because you will have taken your individuated energy to be with ones in other constellations once again where you have known joy and companionship. You have experienced many lifetimes, and much in this lifetime, of being away from home; not only the Home of the Father, the kingdom of the Father, but being away from home where the family was, where the friends were, the companions with whom you journeyed, created, knew oneness together.

You have wanted to return. You have looked to your heavens and you have wondered, "What is up there? Why do I feel drawn to a certain star?" There is a resonance that you feel, even a homesickness, a feeling of, "I think I've been part of that." And then there is a knowing that, "Yes, I have been part of that."

Explorers that you are, adventurers that you are, creative ones that you are, you will be forever seeking new frontiers and bringing forth new galaxies. Even as we speak, you are bringing forth the birth of new stars. You are bringing the involution of the energy of the dark holes, for there are many, right now, of the so-called black holes where the energy is being drawn in upon itself in order to become dense enough to explode once again as light particles into new stars and new galaxies, new frontiers. Will you want to experience what those new frontiers feel like? Of course, you will. That is why you have the courage in this day and time to allow the imagination to expand upon the Isness and the concept of Isness.

Your scientists are beginning to understand. They have questioned the size and nature of the universe; even if it is infinite, they say, it still has to be finite. There must be an edge. There is no edge, because you are pushing the edges all the time. The cosmos is expanding. The universe is expanding, and will continue to expand. That which you are complete with, that which fulfills its purpose, will go back into thought energy and be reborn again, much as you have the seasons of your time, where you have the season of the quiet time, and then there is the spring where the newness of life comes forth and matures and ages and ripens as great fruit to bring forth civilizations that are in awareness of all that they are, all that they can be. And then there is a time when that fruit is harvested, made over into new form in the quiet time to bring forth new life again, forever expanding.

Beyond even the most wonderful concept that you have of time, there is much of awareness, expression, and experience that is outside the sphere of time. That is not to naysay the value of time; there is much value in time itself. But there is within what you see as the Allness of You the concept of time, and the sphere of time is but a small percentage. That is how vast, how wonderful you are. Having said that, I will let you contemplate for a while.

Cross-Culture Multiculturalism

I would share with you now some of the insights I learned in my lifetime. I was privileged to travel to many countries, and I saw, as you see now, the chaos which was happening in the various countries. I saw the chaos which existed in families and how brothers and sisters, even well-meaning ones, were not as loving as they could have been.

I had the experience of knowing many cultures. I grew up as a very small one in Egypt and then in the hometown of Nazareth, and as I grew in the Essene community at Mt. Carmel and as I traveled to study with masters in the Far East, then to what is known now as Great Britain and all throughout what you call the continent of Europe, I came to know the different peoples and cultures, so I had a very broad understanding of a commonality which is important for you to recognize now, the commonality of the divine essence of each one whom you meet.

You will see varying cultures. You see this in your geo-political country. This planet has been an experiment, in a way, to see how various starseeds could work together, how they could evolve into an awareness of Oneness. All of you have come from various star constellations, and sometimes you meet up with ones you feel familiar with. You feel that you are in resonance with them. And then there are others with whom you do not feel a familiarity.

Your country, as it was founded by enlightened ones, was and is an example of co-mingling of cultures to a place where, hopefully, the different cultures can live together in harmony and in respect and even in celebration of some of the differences that the cultures bring. The co-mingling which has happened for the last two centuries of your time in this geo-political country is now happening in many other countries as well, where there are many immigrants coming to lands and either trying to fit in with the culture already established there or establishing themselves as an isolated community within that country.

You are privileged, because of your choice, to be part of this new experiment, this new understanding of at-One-ment. You have chosen, master that you are, to be the starseed who would come to participate in something that is not known in other constellations, other realities. You have chosen, master that you are, to live in this reality and to evolve in this reality and to come to a place where you know yourself to be One with All and in Love with All.

When you meet ones who are of a different perspective, allow yourself to have a discourse with them as to what their belief is, what their traditions are. Why do they believe as they do? Your questioning will help them question why they hold certain beliefs. And the questioning about their beliefs will then allow them to question certain actions, because all actions—hear this well—all actions come out of belief.

Whatever one believes, is going to be the motivating force for whatever choice of action is made. So you will ask of them, "What do you believe about the planet, about other ones who inhabit the planet? What do you believe about the geo-political grouping that you find yourself in? Do you see value in other people's belief systems?" You will ask that; probably nobody has ever asked them that.

They may even ask you what you believe. And as you will speak about your beliefs, it will come easier for you to have a clear understanding of what is fundamental to your belief and your actions and your choices.

You have principles which have been set out by your forefathers, your founding fathers who were enlightened, and you can go back to those principles and ensure that they are enacted by you and by your leaders. You have a voice, and you can use it. It is time now to use it forcefully and yet respectfully; to not sit quietly by when you see abuse of power of any kind.

I was and I am a pacifist, in that I believe in peace, but I also believe in speaking clarity to brothers and sisters so that they have a chance to see where they are coming from. When you see abuse and non-respect of any class of people, speak up. Do not just walk by or cross over the street to the other side, physically or metaphorically. Speak up about it. Know that all is evolving, and that it is going to evolve a lot faster if you take your actions from the principles which you know aid and promote peace.

If you are willing to take those actions, the evolution towards heaven on Earth is going to happen much more quickly. That is where you stand right now; you individually are going to be and have been already called upon to stand up for your belief, and in the days to come you are going to be called upon even more to speak your truth.

Do not be afraid to speak your truth. Separated ego is going to say, "Oh, yes, but I remember another lifetime when I did this and I was outcast from the village, and the wild animals took me as meat. I remember other lifetimes when I spoke out about abuse and the authorities did not like it, and I was asked to give the head over, or I was burned at the stake, etc."

That is not going to happen in this lifetime. You may feel that you get crucified in an emotional sense, because ones are going to perhaps have a reaction to what you say, but that is okay. That does not really touch you. That comes from their own defensiveness. It comes from their own belief about themselves and how they think they have to defend themselves.

You have now a most wonderful cross-culture multiculturalism. You have many cultures that are coming to live next door to your dwelling place. Get to know them. Get to understand why they believe as they do. Know that the choices they make come from their belief system, and allow yourself to help to integrate them into a place of respect for themselves and respect for others.

In my day and time, as I have said, I was very fortunate to have the opportunity to travel to many countries; I had a good travel agent—as you do. He is known as the Holy Self. You have been sent to many different countries and places you have visited, and you know ones who have moved into this country from other places. They come to you at your place of work, in your place of buying your groceries, your place of filling up the energy of the vehicles. You meet them in different social settings.

Speak with them as friend to friend. Let them know what your belief is about the world and what you see as the vision for the future. Let them know what you see as integration of all cultures into one harmonious culture, not losing diversity, but having honor and respect for each one and for each individual member within that grouping. Now, there are some belief systems which do not hold respect within their own cultures for certain members. You will speak from the vantage point of your belief that women, for example, are to be respected. It does not matter what the physical body looks like. What matters is the spirit, the motivating force.

In addition, I was privileged to know many languages. If you know the language of another culture, you are able to understand the belief system a lot easier. The sense of separation falls away if you can understand what they are saying.

In this country you are finding more and more of the immigrants coming with their own languages, and you speak your supposed predominant language, but you hear many different sounds around you. The most wonderful way to come to an understanding with another individual is to know their language. So it is a suggestion that your small ones be taught, either in your schooling places or at home, several languages, as many as possible, so that there can be an understanding of what ones are saying. Then there is not a feeling of separation where you are excluded.

You already have witnessed this as you go through your grocery stores, where ones are speaking to each other in various languages or they are on your most wonderful technology of the telephone and they are speaking to one in another language as they pass you by, and you feel somewhat separate because you do not understand what they are saying. Now, probably they are only asking, "Do you want me to buy the carrots?" but you do not know. It makes for a sense of separation. So start with the small ones and start with yourself in learning the different languages.

The other thing that you can do, and you can start it right away—in fact, you have already—is to develop your sense of intuition. Even if you do not understand what the words mean, tune in to your intuition, that inner knowing of what they may be talking about, what they are saying, what they may be feeling.

If you already speak several languages—there are several that are predominant within this country—learn a new one that may sound Greek to you. Try Greek. It is fun; it is different. Try Russian. Purchase the language tapes. Try understanding the language of your fellow brothers and sisters who live in Iran. Understand what is being said in their own language; not just what is being translated into English, which may be close or not close to what is truly being said or meant.

Allow yourself that edge. Do not sit idly by and say, "Well, Holy Spirit will take care of it." Holy Spirit can only take care of what you take care of, because you are the emissaries of Holy Spirit right here, right now, incarnate. Holy Spirit wants to take care of it, but you have to do it. So go out in this week of your timing and purchase one language, and set aside a few minutes each day to at least listen to it. You do not have to learn it if you do not want to, but at least familiarize yourself with the different sounds.

Do not walk as a stranger in this land any longer. Claim all of the Earth and its languages and its people as your own, because you all are brothers and sisters. You may say, "Well,

I am too old to learn a language. I'm way past being able to make any of those sounds. My tongue doesn't...well, it hardly gets around the English language."

I assure you, as you listen, you will begin to find that the Child of you is alive and well and will want to learn.

When you begin to do that, it will lead to a most wonderful place that you may not be able to envision now, but a place that I can envision for you, because you are going to find yourselves being translators. If you have ever wondered, "What purpose does my life have? Why am I working this certain job? What can I yet do with the years that are ahead of me? What do I really want to do that will fulfill my soul purpose?" play with the vision of being a translator, because it is going to be most necessary as the cultures clash.

The cultures have to integrate, but they are not going to integrate until there is understanding, and there is not going to be true understanding until you can know what the languages are saying. So begin right where you are with what you already know and add unto it. If you are courageous enough, allow yourself to hold the vision that, "I am going to be a translator for some groups."

Many of you have come as first generation immigrants into this country. Many of you saw the parents have to learn the language and to integrate themselves into this country and its values and its ideals.

In some families, they may send the small ones to school where the small ones learn the language that is the common denominator of the country, but at home the old language is spoken. The children of that family are the ones who are the bridge people who can translate, who can make understanding, who can say to the parents, "This is what people are saying, and this is why they are saying it."

There is a globalization which many have railed against, but it inevitable, and the better you understand the brothers and sisters, the easier the transition is going to be and the less the resistance is going to be. Globalization has to happen. Your technology is making it possible now so you can do business with ones halfway around our holy Mother, the Earth, even adjusting for time zones.

Now you have to adjust for languages, understanding that truly that is the next barrier that has to fall. There has to be a cross-cultural integration, and the only way—well, the quickest way—is to be able to speak the language, plus what we have spoken about with the intuition, the open heart.

So I send you forth with a very important message of homework. **Purchase for yourself a set of language tapes in this next week**. And then begin to understand the culture and traditions from which that language has sprung. All of the languages of the various life forms that came as points of Light on holy Mother Earth—starseeds—started out with sound. And the sounds began to be understood by the local grouping, so that the tribe—as it would be called—understood what was being communicated. But perhaps the neighboring tribe did not understand, and this led to warring. You now have bigger tribes, and you still have warrings. But you are evolving.

Do some cross-culture integration and understanding. It will be fun. And when you step out of the usual, you are going to find out more about yourself, and that is going to be enlightening.

Your Lineage

Beloved one, you have a most wonderful lineage. We have spoken in other times of the rainbow and how the vibrations of the rainbow manifest as colors. We have spoken that there is an affinity, a resonance, if you will, that certain ones of you feel with each other.

Sometimes you will meet up with brothers and sisters and there is not quite the closeness or the resonance with them, although you may admire them for what they are doing and how they are living their lives, but it is not the same resonance and not an easy feeling as you have with one who is of same vibration.

Those of you who are waking up now are of the same vibration. You are of the same lineage. You go back to a time before time to a place where there was Thought to create from a knowing of Oneness an out-picturing of harmony in all of creation.

Now, not all of the vibrations have come with the same knowing. This does not make you more special than they are; in other words, you cannot have a rainbow if you do not have all the different vibrations.

You have come with a lineage of knowing the Godself of you, and it has not been forgotten throughout many, many, many eons of time. You have had the incarnations, however you define incarnation, in the different constellations, even the ones that are yet to be discovered.

You have had incarnations on the different planets in this solar system where you have worshiped the sun and you have seen it as symbolic of your divinity, because you have remembered your divinity.

You have not forgotten your divinity. It has been covered over by a temporary forgetting from time to time because you have said that you will walk with the brothers and sisters, the other vibrations of the rainbow. You will walk with them in a place of love, in a place where they can feel comfortable with you.

And so you have temporarily forgotten the divinity, but it is only temporary and it is only a surface forgetting. Deep within you, you do remember your divinity. That is why you get upset sometimes when you see the horrendous unloving acts that occur, either planned or unplanned. That is why you have the heart that is compassionate, a sensitive loving heart that wants to see a time when there will be peace on Earth and ones will love each other.

There is much that is just beyond the consciousness. If you were to envelop, say, the aura around you and to feel that that is the boundary of your knowing, there is much that is in the place of unknowing beyond that. And there is a feeling within you that knows, even without "evidence", even without proof, that there is much more than just the individual life, much more than just the body, much more than the challenges that come with human life, much more than just getting through each day's activities.

There is a knowing born of the lineage that you are part of, a knowing that you have left clues all along the way for remembrance to wake up and to smell the divinity, to feel the divinity. You have clues even on holy Mother Earth that are now under the water, and yet quite visible. Ones have gone deep under the water and have found carvings to the gods who were worshiped in that long-ago culture.

You have certain pyramids that are under water now that were built by you and by the brothers and sisters in a time almost forgotten. Then as the cycle of the holy planet has evolved with the ice melting and the rising of the water—which by the way is a cycle and will be happening again, but not in this lifetime—the water came up and rose over the evidence of the civilization. But it is still there.

As recent as a few years ago when there was the great tsunami in another part of your world, when the water receded in the tsunami out quite a few miles, it exposed a lot of the carvings of the rocks under the water. Photographs were taken of what was under the water and is under the water, so there is evidence/proof of civilization that was there before the waters rose.

Your lineage is one of remembrance. That is why I speak to you so often of remembrance, of coming Home, of touching the place within that remembers divinity. Others of the brothers and sisters have focus upon other things that they feel they have to accomplish or to finish or to complete, because many of the brothers and sisters are completing that which they have felt was incomplete perhaps from eons of time ago when they expressed in a different form or a different location, a different planet or a different constellation.

All life on holy Mother Earth is made up of the starseeds from the other constellations with a history of living on the different planets in this solar system and living on the planetary bodies in other solar systems, the other constellations where you see now the brightest star which is as a sun in another solar system that does have, in many cases, the planets circling about it and does have life that it is sustaining; life perhaps not as you understand this form of life, but life nonetheless.

Allow yourself at least five minutes of your valuable time in every day to contemplate why you are here. Set aside five minutes to breathe deeply. And as you are doing the deep breathing, remember your lineage, bring forth through the breath the remembrance of your connection to the divinity of All—five minutes in every day.

It will be good for the body. It opens up the cells of the body. It allows the lungs to expand. But more than that, you are taking in the divinity of yourself that is all around you, and you are being consciously aware that, "I Am the expression of the creative One. I have a body that I am using in this time. I am not the body, but I do take care of it, and I do acknowledge how powerful it can be in the awakening."

The awakening happens in the consciousness, and you stand in a place now on the threshold of that change, that one snap where you come to a place of realizing with one thought, "I Am divine. I Am from that one creative Source; otherwise, I would not be," and that is true.

And what a difference that realization will make, because you will go out then into the world and the positive feeling, the positive ions that you have activated by the breathing and by the consciousness are going to go out as little molecules — envision that. They are going to go out and they are going to touch other people, and other ones may not know what they are being touched by, but they feel good as you pass by, the same as the grass, the trees, the flowers respond to your energy. Your positive ions go out and touch them, as well. Even your vehicle will respond to the positive ions.

Beloved one, when I look upon you, I see the positive ions. When I look upon you, what I see is the light of you, the aura of you, the radiance of you, the true heart that beats in remembrance of your divinity, the true heart that wants to know the awakening of the collective consciousness.

That is what I have come to say to you.

Positive Ions

Beloved one, to review, you are the expanded expression of divinity, come from the one Source, the one creative One, come forth from before time began to have an experience known as human, to have other experiences that you are now beginning to tap into, and to be the expression of the creative One walking the face of our holy Mother, the Earth.

Know that truly you are One with everything that you see, everything that you feel, everything that you experience. It is your consciousness that brings forth everything you experience. Others have other experiences. Their consciousness is aware of other experiences. Everything that you experience is in your awareness because of your consciousness and because of your desire to remember and to come Home, even while walking on the two feet having the human experience.

From the moment that you thought that there could be otherwise than Oneness, otherwise than divinity, from that moment you decreed that you would live a drama, and so you have created lifetimes of drama. Some of you have practiced so well that you are the drama queens and kings. You know how to play your parts very well. But you also know—as we have talked about this in other times—how to take that holy deep breath, the easy breath that allows you to step into a new space and to feel the peace that the breath brings with it, and to be able to look at whatever is happening with new eyes; not the world eyes, because the world judges and the world usually says you are coming up short with everything, but to be able to look with the holy eyes and to look with love upon yourself and your choices and upon others and their choices and to love them no matter what choices they make.

You have come as a great ray of Light. You have come to share your Light. You have come with a contract that says, "Yes, I will live the life of a human, but I will also begin to remember the expansion of my soul, the expansion of what I have called my individual self," to the place where you see yourself as part of the rainbow that we spoke of earlier, where you can see that you are part of the whole, and yet you are an individual—as you understand individual—vibration of Light, a color, if you will, in the rainbow.

And so you will see that you are expressing that which is needed, that which is called for, that which you have agreed that you will do, even if you do not understand at the time what you are doing.

Allow yourself to live in love. Know yourself to be loved by me. Share with me what is going on. Talk with me. I am not afar off as you have believed for many lifetimes. I am not up on the cross, still hanging on the cross. I am not up there. I am not afar off in some other dimension. I am right here with you every day, every moment. So speak with me as you drive your vehicle. Sing to me. Sing with me. Tell me a joke. I love humor. Allow me to speak to you. Allow me a moment or so to respond before you go on to the next topic.

You have what is called the Lord's Prayer, the "Our Father." Some of you have been raised with it from the time you were very small in this lifetime, and many other lifetimes, as well, so that you have practiced all of the words of the prayer, and there is the contest to see how fast you can get through it.

Allow yourself when you say the Lord's Prayer to think upon each word and its meaning — or to take another prayer, something that is familiar to you that feels divine — and to contemplate the meaning of the words, the meaning that is behind the words. Allow yourself to take even one word into meditation, a time of quiet, to reflect, "What are the aspects of this word? What does it mean to me on the surface as it is usually used? What is the deeper meaning that it symbolizes?"

It is easy to be in judgment. But for those of you who are moving past judgment, take the deep breath whenever the news media brings you breaking news. What does it break? We have spoken of this before: it breaks your peace. That is what breaking news will do. Allow yourself to stand back from it and to acknowledge that there is a brother or sister who does not yet know their divinity, does not yet know the simplicity of being taken care of, not yet knowing that they do not have to toil with all of the mental gymnastics of wondering how they can make their mark and how they can amass more power. They do not yet know that they can allow themselves to be at peace and to live the simple life of just loving and being, and loving the being.

They will come to a place where they will know peace. That which you see them doing now, you recognize, because you have done it yourself in another lifetime. So you do not judge. You only say, "Bless you on your journey."

One of the things you will want to focus upon is the positive energy that you are. There is positive energy that you put forth as you are happy. There are little bubbles of positive ions that exude from you, from your being, when you are happy, when you are smiling, when you know you are whole, when you are in a place that recognizes that you are loved.

You put forth little bubbles that can be seen by some ones. They are positive ions. They are ones that can be photographed. You have the technology for photographing the aura around you; you have already seen that. The positive ions can be photographed, as well, and they allow the vibration around you to be uplifted.

Many of you have prayed for ascension. Many of you have said, "I want to be an ascended master." I speak unto you that you *are* the ascended master; otherwise, that concept would not be within your realm of knowing. You are an ascended master. You have been, in other lifetimes, in the place of ascension where you have recognized how it feels to rise above all worldly cares.

This lifetime you have said, "I will be closer to some of the worldly cares so that I can raise up the ones who do not know that there is something else." And so you have come a bit closer to the worldly outlook of things, yet remembering deep within you the divinity and the positive ions that you truly are as energy.

All is energy, and as you will accentuate the positive ions, it allows an ascension of consciousness—your consciousness first, because you are the one who is living in the midst of the positive bubbles of ions, and also the collective consciousness as it is touched by the energy. As you will focus upon the positive ions and allow yourself to live in positive energy, you give out the energy to a place where others can be touched by it and be encouraged by it. Over the last few decades of your timing, there has been a growing focus on awakening, on meditation, ideas such as the peace clock where ones will focus on peace instead of the negative ions.

Over the last few decades the positive energy has been growing to a place where you have many ones who bring forth the message of ascension, ascending for a moment or so out of the worldly cares, sometimes ascending for an hour, even for a day, a week, or perhaps longer.

It is happening right now. You have a feeling of hope, a feeling of, "Perhaps this can happen. Perhaps I can be part of this." Well, of course, you can be part of it. You are already doing it. "Perhaps I can allow collective consciousness to feel an upliftment and to bring about the Awakening, to bring about the knowing where ones feel good about themselves once again." More and more of your lecturers, your writers, the ones who are giving forth messages are inundating the collective consciousness with positive ions, and there is an awakening that is happening.

And you are part of it, because you have agreed before the incarnation that you wanted to make impact, you wanted to be here to experience what it would feel like to be in a very dense place—and you have experienced denseness. You have felt the dark night of the soul where you literally did not sleep because there was a darkness that you felt was going to overwhelm and overcome you, and maybe you would not even be able to breathe; and yet you did.

Then you came to the place where there is the dawning, the literal dawning of the next morning. It did happen, much to your surprise, because you thought, "I am going to expire during this night. It is too much to handle."

And yet you kept one breath after another, and the next morning did come; not only the literal morning, but the figurative morning, where you began to say, "Wow, you know, I've come through that dark night of the soul, and boy, was it heavy! I was really, really afraid. I didn't think I was going to survive it. But, you know, I did survive it. And if I survived it, I must be more powerful than I thought I was. There must be something within me that's keeping me going."

Well, there is. It's your divinity. It is the power of the divine One that has said, "I'm not finished yet. I have work to do." And so the morning dawns and you allow even in that morning a few of the positive ions to go forth from you, a feeling of relief, perhaps.

So I charge you with the task, which is a very happy task, of being the positive ions, and I remind you not to spend too much time with the negative ions. I know that they come forth. They are part of duality, but you do not have to live in that space. You can acknowledge them. You can even make great drama around them, and then you are finished.

Have you ever recognized that when you are in a place of the negative ions and you feel like everything is coming crashing down on you and you are the worst example of human being that there ever could be and everything is totally wrong with you — you are too big, too small, too unknowing, too stupid, too whatever separated ego will say to you — and you feel yourself to have made many mistakes and to be the most unlovable, and you cry, you cry your heart out and you lose yourself in those sobs, have you ever noticed that after awhile the sobs finish?

You have expended all of the negative ions that you have, and they are gone. What is left is peace. You have been at that place where you have cried and cried and cried and screamed and you have said, "This is terrible. What I am experiencing and how I feel about myself is terrible. I am the worst example of human being. How could I ever be divine? I am not divine," and you have denied your divinity.

And you have sobbed and cried and thrown things and been quite the drama person. But then there comes a place where you are finished. There comes a place where you breathe. Finally you breathe. You breathe in the positive ions that have always been around you. You breathe them out in peace, because you are finished with the negative.

And then you begin to dance, sometimes quite literally, always figuratively, because you have found that no matter how harshly you judge yourself, no matter how much turmoil you put the body through with all of the sobs and screams, even to the place where you lose the voice, you come to the place of recognizing that, "I Am that which I have always been. I Am that which I Am. I Am truly indestructible."

At that point of remembrance, when ones would take a photograph of you with special lens, they would be able to see the positive ions—known as orbs—around you. Now, not all orbs are your own positive ions. Some orbs are the loved ones, the masters, the ones who have decided to be light orbs and to remind you of your Light. They are in a space of positivity, of being the positive ions.

Accentuate the positive ions as often as you can remember. When you get into a negative space, recognize it for what it is. If you desire to stay in that space for awhile, know that it will spend itself and be finished. Allow yourself then to come up out of that negative space and to be in a positive ionic space, because it feels good.

Have you ever been with ones who were laughing about something and you did not know what they were laughing about, but that laughter was so contagious that you found yourself laughing with them? Ones will start a laugh and it goes around, and you get caught up in it and you accentuate the positive.

You have a saying in one of your musical songs, I believe, to "accentuate the positive, eliminate the negative, and don't mess with mister in between." You see, I listen. (Smile)

Allow yourself to put forth the positive ions everywhere you go. Give a smile; it costs nothing, and it feels good. And sometimes it will surprise others and they will wonder what you are smiling about. It spreads. It is contagious.

Allow others to know that there is another way to look at everything. They do not have to choose it. If they want to dwell with the negative ions for awhile, know that they are doing the completion with whatever they feel they have to complete.

Truly, everything is complete and they can be happy right now and live in positivity, but sometimes they do not feel complete with whatever the situation may be. So you smile at them, and they frown at you, because how can you smile when they are going through such a tough time? But you smile at them and you allow the positive ions to grow and to uplift all of humanity, including yourself. Accentuate the positive.

Fifth Dimensional Perspective

Now, because the times are changing, there is much of awareness that is going to be needed in the next few years, of knowing that your belief system really does alter that which you find yourself experiencing.

Allow yourself to live in 5th dimensional innocence often: the place of taking the deep breath, and the place of peace that knows that always you are taken care of. There is nothing and no one who can challenge you or make you have an experience that you cannot call good.

I know that there are many in the world who will challenge that statement, because there is much that is going on in the world that does not look to be good. You have, from time to time on the world stage, occurrences which are called disasters—and the word "disaster" is really indicative; truly, it means "that which comes from the stars"; dis-aster; something that you long, long time ago, as you would see yourself to be the ancestors, thought that if any so-called tragedy happened, it was from the gods in the heavens; the stars sent this down here for you to have an experience called a dis-aster—from the stars.

But truly, you manifest everything that you experience, and if you call it disaster, stop for a moment and realize that you are from the stars, as well. Truly, many of you have said that Mother Earth is not your home. It is not your home planet, but you did help and are helping as co-creators to sustain Gaia, Mother Earth, for the time being to fulfill a purpose of many incarnations and many evolutionary changes. But you are from the stars yourself, and so in truth, you are a dis-aster—in the best way. (Smile)

All of you as small children had the feeling and said to your parents at one time or another, "Where's Home?" And your mother or father said, "Well, it's right here." And you said, "No, this is not Home." And because they did not want to deal with the feelings which that would bring up, they said, "Oh, that's rubbish. You *are* home; forget that." They also knew the feeling of being displaced, but they did not know how to deal with it, so therefore they would deny it.

All of you have felt different, not at Home, but you *have* volunteered to be here to help with bringing in the consciousness of 5th dimension, bringing in the consciousness of peace and innocence. And when you live in that consciousness of peace and innocence, it leads to a most wonderful gift known as joy: Joy that the world does not know.

You, at the soul level, have already chosen what you term your future. Now, some of the details of it have been left to your choosing, but at the soul level you have set certain parameters and goals that you want to do and will do in this lifetime. The details are up to you, but the overall plan, your soul's plan, you set for yourself before the incarnation, and you will accomplish it, so you might as well sit back and relax and enjoy it.

Separated ego says, "Oh, but I have to plan, I have to know where I'm supposed to go, what I'm supposed to do. I have to know all the details, because something might be lurking in my future that I don't want to be there, and I have to be prepared to deal with it."

We have spoken to you in previous times of being the Beholder, taking the deep breath and standing back from whatever is going on and just watching the interplay of all of the circumstances, all of the options and the people involved.

Fifth dimensional perspective goes one degree further than that. Fifth dimensional perspective calls it all good and says, "I don't have to do it." You have a saying in your holy Scriptures attributed to me, that "I of myself do nothing," and that is true. You of the small self, the separated ego, you can do a whole lot of running around, scurrying here and there, reading all the books, quoting all of the "masters", and worrying, but the true Self of you already knows 5th dimensional perspective where you are already in synch with your soul's plan, and that is the plan that you are going to live.

I have seen you wrestling with decisions and wondering what you should do and trying out various options: "How does this feel, how does that feel, should I do this, should I do that?" You spend a lot of energy worrying. But I have also seen you take a deep breath and say, "Oh, what the heck. I'm living the Now moment, and right now nobody is threatening me and right now I'm okay. I think I'll stay here right now for another Now moment."

If you keep on doing that, guess what happens. You keep living in the Now moment of being okay and being taken care of, being guided to make the decisions that fit the soul's plan. Do not turn yourself upside down trying to figure out what is the best solution.

Before any incarnation, you put together a plan that is going to bring about the best for you and for the brothers and sisters with whom you are going to be interacting. You set up appointments with other ones that you will meet with them at a certain time in the lifetime and that you will work together with them on certain projects.

Before the incarnation you set up a general plan of how you are going to heal yourself; in other words, remember your wholeness and how you are going to heal others by your interaction with them. It may be sometimes with a bit of challenge and require tough love, which does not always feel the easiest way, but it is what you have agreed that you will do, and you need never be in turmoil with yourself.

When the world is too much with you—and I know how the world will clamor, how the disasters are reported to you and you feel that everything out there and everything in your own immediate vicinity is looking like it *could* be really bad and you feel the world is screaming at you—take yourself, if it is possible, physically out into nature and be One with the process of Life itself, with the trees, the bushes, the grass, the flowers, and see how they do not worry, "Am I

143

going to have enough rain? Enough sunlight?" They only know life process.

A tree does not know death. A tree does not worry about death. A tree knows only to live. If someone comes along and cuts down the tree, the tree does not agonize over what has happened. The life force is still in that wood, as my father Joseph has reminded you. The life force is still in the wood, no matter how it is fashioned or how it is used. Even if it is used as kindling for the fireplace and it is burned, it turns into the energy that truly Life force is. Nothing is ever lost. And so the tree does not worry about being lost, because that possibility is never in its computer program.

Now, humankind loves to make complexity, because you are creative. So you create, and you ask, "What can I create that is unlike the Truth of my being?" And you are very good at creating all kinds of experiences. Separated ego then says, "See, here is evidence. The world is not a safe place to be. The world is a place where you have to struggle." But that is *separated* ego.

When you allow the deep breath and you go to the place of 5th dimensional peace and innocence, you look upon what has been happening and you see how it serves the bigger picture, what I have called the at-One-ment, the realization of Oneness, the realization of how divine and how creative you are. If, and when, you can allow yourself to be in that space and to say, "Wow, I am really creative; look at this mess I have made," then you have made it. In other words, you have graduated to the place where you can congratulate yourself on your creativity and call that good.

That is 5th dimensional perspective. It is where I would abide as often as possible. When the world would be too much with me, I took myself apart to pray. I took myself physically into nature. And always, if it is not possible to do this physically, you can do it on the emotional level of taking the deep breath. Even if you are surrounded by all of chaos around you, all of the quarreling co-workers, all of the world that seems to be judging itself and finding itself to be wrong, emotionally you can withdraw from that and take yourself apart from it. You take the deep breath, you put the smile on the face and know that you are always taken care of.

You need not worry about the golden coins. Always you will have enough golden coins. You have proved that to yourself already in this lifetime. Sometimes you have come to the place where you have not had two golden coins to rub together, and you have wondered, "Oh, gosh, what's going to happen?" And then someone comes along, and they may not give you golden coins, but they give you a loaf of bread, so you did not even have to go through the process of going to the store and buying the bread. Someone did all that for you and gave you the loaf. Then you may be tempted to say, "Oh, that's great for now, but where's my next meal coming from?"

That is separated ego not living in 5th dimension when it starts to worry about the future. Live in the Now. Look around you to see what you have in the Now. Right now you have raiment. You have had food. You have friends, perhaps near, perhaps far. You have work that you like to do, or not. If you do not like your work, who says you have to stay with it? You can change it.

The wonderful part about being creative is that you can morph; you can change; you can even change the circumstances around you. If you are not happy with the circumstances around you, start envisioning, "What would I like the circumstances to be? How would it feel?"

You are going to morph; you are going to change. The world is going to change. The world is in a place now where it has come up against the brick wall where choices have to be made, and some of those changes are going to be seen, at first, to be threatening.

Trust. Breathe peace. Know that truly you are always guided. You have touched the place of 5th dimension. You know what it feels like, even if it was a bit tenuous, even if it just came for a moment or so where you felt a peace that you had not known before, and within a moment of recognizing it and feeling it, then it was gone because you were not accustomed to that peace. But if you have once felt it—and you have—you can feel it again, and you can bring it back.

All is energy, as we have spoken many times, and if you will live in the energy of joy and trust, others will pick it up from you. "You mean that's contagious, too?" Oh, yes, it is not just the negative things that are contagious. Joy, laughter, light-heartedness in the face of confusion are contagious, and it feels really, really good to let all of the worries of separated ego be forgotten and left behind for awhile.

You can always go back and pick up the worries if you want to, but having left them behind for awhile and having lived in the place of joy and trust and knowing that you are guided, you are not going to want to go back and pick up all the worries of separated ego, even if separated ego says to you that you are responsible for doing such and such.

So whenever you see what is called the disaster, whenever you see the world seemingly going through trials and tribulations, count it all as good and say, "Yes, I agreed to that." You may be wide-eyed about it and say, "Wow, I agreed to *that*?" Yes, you agreed to that because you knew the light at the end of the tunnel.

Now, I know it is a little more difficult to trust when you are incarnate. When you are discarnate and you are looking at the overall plan, you can see how all the puzzle pieces fit together and you can say yes to it, which is what you did.

When you are in the midst of it, it is a bit like being lost in the forest and you see many trees around you and you are not quite sure which way is *out* of the forest. But you do trust that there is a way to get through the forest, and you bless every tree along your way. It is a bit of a challenge to live in trust, but you bless every tree in the forest and you know that you are going to come out the other side of it, and when you look back at the forest, you are going to say how blessed that forest is, because you blessed every tree as you went through it.

Allow yourself to practice living in 5th dimensional perspective, the place of the heart; not the mental—that is separated ego—but the place of the heart that trusts, that knows peace even in the midst of chaos, that knows innocence and freedom from worry, knows that truly everything does work together for good—as you judge good to be—everything works for the realization of harmony and Oneness.

Live in that space. Allow it to be contagious. Even speak words to some who may be doubting, and yet they invite you to speak a word to them that may be a bit unconventional in the world's thinking. It is okay; you can shake them up a bit. They will either accept it or not. That is not your responsibility. But allow yourself to be at peace, because everything truly is working out in divine order to bring humankind back to the realization of the power of the one holy innocent Child.

And as I have said, when you see things that seem to be otherwise, call them good, because you have agreed to them as wake-up calls. That is okay. You can roll with them, and you can be okay because you have found your heart.

Live from the heart. Allow the head, the mental, to serve the heart. Use 5th dimensional peace and perspective to guide you and to keep you.

Starseeds of the Future

Beloved one, you are in training. Did you know this? You have agreed that you will incarnate to be *in* the world, but not *of* the world. You have agreed that you will serve the divinity of you while wrestling sometimes with the challenges of the world. And, you have agreed that you will make demonstration of the Light, and the joy of the Light.

You have come as a starseed from other planets, other constellations. This is not your first incarnation anywhere, and it is not your first incarnation upon holy Mother Earth. You have volunteered, in what you would see in linear time to be a long, long time ago, to come to bring a remembrance of divinity, of wholeness, and to walk amongst the brothers and sisters—who may be from different cultures and are from different star constellations—to bring your culture, your knowing, your remembrance to bear upon whatever challenge seems to be happening at the time.

You have seen that there are many different cultures in the world at this time, and you have seen ones approach life from generational teaching, what the ancestors have taught and have said was of value and should be revered. You have seen ones go toe to toe, sword to sword, and now with other technology to try to preserve what they have felt was important in generational thinking; in other words, in their culture, because they are from other constellations which knew other ways of being.

You are a starseed of Light. You have come from a planetary mass that knew Light and knew itself to be Light, and you desire to know that again. That is why you seek. That is why you pray. That is why you read the books that you read. That is why you go to the teachers and the workshops.

You remember how it feels to live in harmony. You remember how it feels to be in Light and to feel light; even on the physical level to feel lighter than air and to know that you are the creative One who creates every experience. And yet sometimes you bump up against the world and you wonder, "How can I feel the Light at this time in this circumstance?"

Then you take the deep breath and you come to a place of peace within yourself that then opens a door to the remembrance that you are much more than the body, much more than the personality, much more than all of the books that you have ever read, much more than even what your teachers tell you.

Your teachers are great because they give you clues. They push you. They nudge you, sometimes in reverse psychology. They are very good teachers. The experiences that you bring to yourself are very good teachers, even though sometimes those experiences may feel scarier than death itself. But the experiences are teachers to allow you to come up over, to ascend to a place of knowing the Light that you are.

You have fashioned the body out of the energy of the Light that you are, and you have fashioned the body with a most wonderful piece of equipment that secretes a chemical that when you are in drama you get very excited about it. It is called adrenaline. You seek the adrenaline rush because it allows you to feel alive. It allows you to feel more energized than the usual mundane feeling of daily life. So therefore you seek out drama for the sheer joy of it, for the adrenaline rush. It is a good way for you to access more of the Christ creative energy that you are. It can be addictive to always seek out drama, but if used in a positive way, it is a good clue to the remembrance of how powerful you are as an extension of the one Creator.

As a starseed of Light you have come through many of the different cultures and many of the different centuries, as you measure the linear time. You have come through what has been called the Dark Ages where the main goal was to sustain the body, to exist, to be able to come to a certain point in that lifetime and then release the body, hopefully easily.

You have played *with* everything and *as* everything that you can imagine. You have the computer programs in you for all of the experiences of anything you can imagine. You can call it up seemingly as imagination, and yet if you can imagine it, you have already lived it.

Your science fiction, as it is called, is a most wonderful doorway to remembering what you have done as you would measure the linear time, what you have done in the past and what you may want to move into in the future, or not.

You are in training to come up over the belief in duality, the belief in darkness. You are in training as the starseed of Light to come to the place of realization of the lightness of you; not only the Light as the Christ Light, but as lightness—to take yourself lightly.

Do not worry about the morrow. Do not worry about what the world is going to say to you. Do not worry about what the co-workers and the friends, acquaintances are going to think of you. Their judgment is passing and fleeting and it is arbitrary. As you have seen throughout the centuries of different cultures, that which was deemed to be most beautiful and most desirable changes. It is arbitrary and temporary.

But as a starseed of Light you have come with that little bit of Light within you that remembers how it feels to live in Light, how it feels to live in innocence, no judgment; just to be, and to be joyful in the being because it is so free. As a starseed of Light, you are in a most wonderful playground called the world, a wonderful place to try out various techniques of remembrance, various rituals, various teachings to see which ones resonate and bring forth the most light feeling within you. That is what you are seeking to know. You want to know freedom from the shackles of the world, the shackles of darkness, the shackles that say there has to be suffering.

You have had generational teaching that has taught you that the more you suffer in this life, the more your reward in the hereafter. Well, I say unto you, that is not how it works. You do not have to suffer. The hereafter is going to be what you make it, and the Now is going to be what you make it. So therefore, choose lightly.

Choose your thoughts. You have control over your thoughts. Yes, I know that the news media loves to play with your thoughts, loves to report to you all of the machinations of the leaders and the ones who are seemingly in power; the media loves to bring you the news of fresh disasters and to ask you to judge them.

You have choice as to what you will allow within your house, your mind. You have choice whether to dwell upon what was said to you, what may happen tomorrow, what you have to have ready for tomorrow, etc. You know all of those feelings. You do not have to live in a struggle within the mind.

No one controls you. Ones can suggest, but in the end you are the one who makes choice, so choose lightly. There is nobody who is going to come back and have power over you to say that you chose wrongly. Now, separated ego will love to play that script with you. But truly, every choice that you make brings a wealth of experience to you. Every choice that you make gives you more knowledge about results. If you had not chosen whatever it was that you chose, you would not know what was down that road.

As a starseed of Light, your divine birthright is to live in Light, to take yourself lightly, and to allow others to feel lighter when they are with you. That is your assignment, and you may take it or not. In other words, the choice is up to you. But you have found that as you go through a day feeling happy about something, feeling that you are truly okay—because you are—others can feel your joy, your happiness, and then they are uplifted.

You have a saying in your holy Scriptures that, "I, if I be lifted up, will draw all men unto me"—women, as well. I, if I be lifted up in my consciousness, lifted up into that Christ knowing, lifted up into love which is unconditional and unbounded, I will draw all men—and women—unto me to that place of higher consciousness. And then you go with a lighter step. The ones around you can feel lighter, as well, because you are not putting forth the heaviness of the world.

You have come from many other constellations, many other planetary bodies, a long, long time ago, so long ago that you can barely remember it, and yet it is true. You, as a small one, have said to the parents, "Where is home?" And the parents have said, "Well, right here; you're home." "No, that's not what I mean. Where is home? I want to go Home."

Truly, anywhere you are, you are home, because you *are* Home. You carry it within you. You seek outside of yourself that which you carry with you all the time. You seek in the books and the teachers, the gurus, the friends, "Teach me, tell me who I am." And all the while you carry it within you, the Love that you are, the power that you are, the simplicity of Who you are.

No matter how you want to fashion it—and you fashion it different ways in different lifetimes—you *are*, right now, all that you will ever be. So I would suggest—and it is only a suggestion—that you begin to get to know yourself. Begin to take stock of all of the good qualities—as separated ego would judge good and not so good—and then take stock of all of the other qualities that perhaps you would judge to be not so Christ-like or not so good and begin to see how *they* serve, because all of your qualities serve the realization that comes with that divine "Aha!"

Allow yourself, even in this evening, before and as you put the head upon the pillow, to take a deep breath and to say to yourself, "Hey, you know, I'm alive; therefore, there must be some divinity about me. Maybe what I've been seeing of myself is just the tip of the iceberg. Maybe my divinity is within, within my consciousness, within me, and I can choose my thoughts. Wow! I think I'll sleep on that." And you will. You will sleep well.

I can say unto you with surety and a guarantee, you will not have another incarnation like this, because *you* are not going to be the same. You are probably going to choose another incarnation — not necessarily on holy Mother Earth — and you are going to be a starseed of Light fully realized in that incarnation and in the incarnations to follow. That is why I call you a starseed of the future.

That is why you are going through what seems to be rigorous training in this lifetime, so count it all as good—everything. You are past the boot camp. You did that a long, long time ago. You are into what you would call some of the advanced teachings, and yet the only teaching that really matters is coming to know yourSelf—capital "S"—knowing with a conscious awareness that, "I AM all that I will ever be; the love that I am, the power that I am, the creative expression of the divinity. That is who I am, and that is what I am going to be, always. I may out-picture it differently in different incarnations and different experiences, but that will be for the adventure of it." And you do love adventure.

All that you will ever be, all that you *can* be, all that you *want* to be, you *are* right now. Take that deeply within the consciousness and celebrate it. It is no mere thing. Separated ego says that cannot be, but what does separated ego know except separation from the All That Is? So whenever separated ego comes and speaks to you—and it knows you well, it knows all of the little buttons to push—you thank it and say, "Okay, you're excused. You've read your part of the script. Now let me get on with something else that feels better."

Get to know yourself. Celebrate yourself. Allow yourself to live, knowing the radiance of the Light that you have brought to this plane. Allow yourself to believe in the best of yourself, to believe in the best of each other, to believe in the best of all of the happenings. Every disaster, so-called, is an opportunity to look beyond the appearances of it and to see the Light in it.

You are the Light. Why is it that when you see the paintings of me, there is usually a great light around me? It is the same around you. All of the "enlightened" ones who have been portrayed in the paintings have what is called the halo light around them. It is also around you.

Let your Light shine. Look in the mirror and behold the Light that you are. See yourself as I see you. Know that you have purpose. Know that always you will be that which you are, the Light come forth to express and to experience the divinity of you, beloved Starseed of Light.

Visionaries

Beloved one, you are a visionary. You visualize, you envision everything in your life: what is going to happen in the next moment, what is going to happen in the next day, what is going to happen perhaps in the next year. You are visualizing, envisioning what you think will be, most often predicated upon what has been.

Generational teaching has molded you in a certain way, and yet the soul of you knows freedom; the soul of you knows improv; the soul of you knows that so-called reality and perceptions do not have to be the way they have always been according to generational teaching. You visualize according to habit, and if it is a habit, it can be changed.

If what you are visualizing could not be changed, you would not be who you are. But you are divinely empowered to do the improv, as I call it. Even upon a moment's notice you change your mind and you do something else. You have the power of choice. You have the power to change any of the habits that you have developed throughout this lifetime and other lifetimes. That is power, divine power, where you are not stuck in what you have been told is truth—lower case "t". You are not stuck in what you have thought yourself to be or who you have thought yourself to be or what the peers and the parents and the grandparents have told you that you are. You have the power to change, and that is very much what you are doing.

This year in your timing is going to be a powerful year of change—we have spoken of change several years back, because it has been a process ongoing that has started even before this lifetime. Truly, you have descended into density as far as you will ever go, and you are very much on your way back up, ascending, and the ascension is a process, as well. You have declared lifetimes ago that you had reached the bottom of the density. You had gone as far as you wanted to go into the density and into the struggle and into the challenges, and you decided, "There must be something else that I can experience. There must be something else that I can create." And with that thought, you changed everything; a very powerful thought. And from that moment, which was in time according to this linear reality, you have been ascending; sometimes with a great leap of faith, other times a smaller step, but always changing and ascending.

Oftentimes when one will speak of changes, the separated ego says, "Oh, no. Change probably means something that I'm not going to be comfortable with," and fear runs onstage very fast. But the changes I speak of are changes in ascension, and they are good. They are changes that perhaps, at first, separated ego is going to judge as being a bit of a challenge, but that will be only temporary, and it is going to then move into a place where you see the goodness of it.

Separated ego claims its value in fear, but you are not separated from your Source, you are not separate from your divine power of choice, and you are not separate from your power of visualizing what you want your future, your present, your Now to be. You have the power—no one else—and the final decision always comes back to you. It is always your choice.

You have the power to visualize. Now, habitual visualizing is just that. It is based on habit, and it is based on seemingly past evidence of what happens and what is likely to happen. You have met brothers and sisters who go through this lifetime knowing that everything that could possibly be wrong is going to happen, and they are looking for all the things that are going to be wrong. And what happens when you look for something? You find it. And they do find it, and then they say to you, "See, I told you so."

On the other hand, you have your optimists who are happy and they say, "This is going to be one of the greatest days of my life. I know that something good is going to happen in this day. I'm going to meet somebody who is going to tell me something that I've been waiting to hear. I don't know who they are or how this is going to happen exactly, but I'm going to meet them this day." And even before they get out of bed, they put forward their energy into that day, attracting to themselves the people who are going to be in a good space. You can do that. You have that power.

Even before you put the feet on the floor, just pause for a moment, even while the eyes are still trying to open and you still feel sleepy. Allow your consciousness to go forward in the day and imagine, "Who am I going to meet today? What are they going to tell me? How is it going to be?" If separated ego runs in there first, and it often will, say to separated ego, "Okay, I know your story. I want a new story. Today I am going to meet someone who is going to say something to me that is going to light up my world; not only that, but today I'm going to meet someone and I'm going to say something to them that I haven't rehearsed, but it's going to be exactly what they want to hear deep within themselves that is going to enlighten their day."

You have seen in your world over the last few years, even decades, divisiveness among people, and you have been seeing how ones take pleasure in being divisive, in taking the other side of things and standing in whatever they see the opposition could be, taking great pleasure in what they see the game to be. Now, it *is* a game, but they do not understand the stakes of the game. The stakes of the game are the ascension or the temporary halting of the ascension.

You stand at a most pivotal, wonderful place, because you are the visionary: you do visualize from one point of view or another what is going to happen in the next moment, the next day, and the days to come. You often take it for granted because it is usually a habitual way of looking at things, but now you know it does not have to be that way.

As I have suggested in *A Course in Miracles*, "I am determined to see things differently." You can see anew, a new way of thinking, a new way of living. And I tell you, in this time right now — take it to heart — you have the power, the power of choice. If you do not like what you are visualizing and you do not like what seems to be the "evidence" around you, you can change it.

Look for the good. Give forgiveness to the ones you would judge, because after all, they are going to have to forgive you, or have forgiven you for something that you did in another incarnation, because you have been where they are and you have done what they are choosing to do. That is why you recognize what they are doing. There is the computer program in your computer that says, yes, you have been there, done that, and you recognize this as some of your brothers and sisters make choices.

So begin—first off when separated ego runs onstage and says, "Oh, that's bad. That shouldn't be happening. That's not going to be good"—start with forgiveness, the forgiveness that says, "I understand. I've been there. I know." And then you go on from that place with positive replacement, positive visualization of what you want it to be.

What do you love? I ask you this as a question. Think of one thing, person, being, beloved pet; what do you love? You can think of something that you love. How does that make you feel? Expansive, like you can breathe. So when someone is doing something that seems to be something that you could judge, very quickly think of that which you love and how that feels. Ah! That feels good. And that energy, the vibration of that energy — because you are a physical being and you live in energy; that is what you are as you express physically — that energy goes out and expands; it goes out like the ripples on the pond and touches other ones, and may make a difference in the choices they make.

You have been steadily guiding yourself into a new space, and I commend you for that. You have been encouraging others to look at their issues and to forgive the issues and themselves for what has seemed to be judgment, for what has seemed to be harsh and cruel. You have known cruelty; you know it well; well enough that you can now be complete with it. You have known sorrow, loss, and abandonment to the depths of your being, to the place where if you want to touch that space, it is very easy to push that button and be right back in the space of great sorrow and loss. And yet you have worked with coming up out of that space, and you have done well.

However, to live in the space of love all of the time has yet to be realized in this incarnation, in this point of the evolution of ascension.

That is your assignment, should you choose to accept it, and I will help you. Go deep within yourself and ask, "What is most important to me? When I get to the place of releasing the body and I look back on this incarnation, what is going to be most important to me? Is it going to be the golden coins that I saved? Is it going to be the mansion? Is it going to be the vehicle, the automobile? Is it going to be the travel that I have done?" What is going to be most important that you take with you out of this incarnation? What *can* you take with you out of an incarnation? Ponder that for awhile, because the tangible things stay here.

The intangible is what you take with you: the love, the knowing of self-worth, the knowing that a lifetime is truly a reality of love, even though the illusion of fear seems very strong. What you take with you when you release the body are the intangible aspects of you, and those intangible aspects of you grow. Once you have released the body, you expand into the Light and the love of understanding that everyone is lovable, everyone is truly whole, everyone in any circumstances, any situation, is already whole, and even the situation is whole, because it brings forth creativity.

So lay up for yourself in the place called heaven the intangibles—love and expansion, the knowing of self-worth, the knowing that truly everything is in its own divine order. And when you do that, the expansion that you feel when you release the body is going to be as a burst of a constellation of stars, the Light that you are. You have a concept about releasing the body and going through a tunnel to the light. The Light that you go to is your own Light. It is the expansiveness of your own Light. As you very rapidly go through that tunnel and you come to the Light, everything you have ever treasured is there waiting for you: the love that you have always wanted; the loved ones whom you have missed since they laid down the body and released the old shell of the body, they are waiting for you; they are right there, and it is a great reunion, a remembrance of Oneness: re-union.

You have signed a contract that says you will participate in the ascension of the collective consciousness of mankind/womankind/humankind. You have said that you will come and allow your Light to expand to the place where others catch a glimpse, that they can see things differently, that they can *be* different.

Visionaries—you can begin now. Think upon the morrow. What do you plan to do tomorrow? How is it going to go? Are there going to be challenges, or is it going to be easy? Are you going to see everyone as your friend? Are you going to go smoothly through the day, even thanking the weather? Sometimes that can be a bit of a challenge.

Are you going to look upon the holiness of a raindrop, a snowflake, the sunshine, a blade of grass, a tree; to behold the beauty of the way a tree grows? It does not contemplate dying. It does not even contemplate the next moment. It just lives. Why do you bother so much in worrying about what could be wrong or what could happen that you would not like? Why bother yourself by worrying?

Visualize the positive. Visualize the world consciousness awaking, ascending in divine awareness. See each brother and sister reaching out to help one another, recognizing the Oneness that they are, and yet appreciating the uniqueness of each one's talents. You have the choice. Every moment is your choice. Choose you where you will abide. Choose you this day to serve the Christ, the true Self.

The Ascension of the Collective Consciousness

I desire now to continue our conversation about the evolution of consciousness and the evolution of awakening. We have spoken to you how you have, as a collective human consciousness, been at the most dense place. You descended into the greatest density that you could imagine because you wanted to know, "How does it feel to create that which is unlike divine?"

Gradually you came up out of first dimension density, the heaviest, thinking, "There must be something else that I can experience. There must be something that is easier, more rewarding than what I am experiencing."

And so with that thought, with that one glimpse that there might be something different, you moved into second dimension reality, into a place that was not quite as dense, but was still full of challenges and not awake, not even having a glimpse for a long time that there could be something beyond that.

And then again there came the thought, "What more can I create? What can be different than this?" And you moved into third dimensional reality, which is where your world now abides. The collective consciousness, for the most part, is in third dimension.

Now you have ideas, remembrances, urges within yourself to see what else there might be: "Perhaps I can live in peace and in friendship with my brothers and sisters. Perhaps I can live in a space of health; health of body, health of mind, health of friendships and relationships. Perhaps I can be the love that I've heard about." Every time that thought comes up in your mind, you move into fifth dimensional possibilities.

You still have the feet in third dimension, because there is much that you have to take care of in the world, so you do not deny the world. When I was here two thousand years ago, I did not deny the world. I saw the appearances of brother against brother. I saw the cruelty. I saw the judgment. I saw the anger and the jealousy. But I also saw the divinity of brothers and sisters. I also saw the potential of the Christ to live and be expressed by each one of the brothers and sisters, including the ones who seemed to be in opposition.

I knew the potential of the Christ to come alive. That is where you stand now. You know that there is potential for ones to resolve their opposition and their separation from each other. You know, although you do not see it yet, that it is possible that ones can live side by side in peace, even though they may not believe in the same set of ideas, but yet they can allow ones to have differences. When you do that, you move into an expansive place for yourself and also for the collective consciousness.

Fourth dimension occurs when there is that glimpse of the possibility that there could be something more expansive, different than what the parents, the peers, the ones who are seemingly in control have told you that life has to be. As you ponder that possibility, you ask it to be a probability. As you believe in the probability with the intent that it become manifest, it becomes the reality.

So you stand now at a most wonderful place, because you know the possibility and you have the intent to know the probability. The more you focus on something, the more real it becomes for you and to you.

Ones are seeking, as you are seeking. There are many groups all over the face of our holy Mother Earth who are asking to see something different than what they have been brought up to believe in; to see peace, love, friendship, respect; to know compassion.

Over the eons of time that our holy Mother Earth has known life, there have been civilizations which have come alive in their awakening. You know some of these in your history, mainly in mythological and legendary history. Ones living now say, "Oh, yes, those are just stories. Lemuria is just a story." Well, it is a story, but it is also and was a reality, and many of you lived in Lemuria. Many of you knew the vibration of nature in Lemuria, and you worshiped it in Oneness because you knew yourself to be the vibration of nature, and you knew how to encourage the plants, the trees, the vegetation, the mountains to grow, to speak to you. You knew Oneness of communication. And so, Lemuria fulfilled its contract.

Atlantis had another focus of attention, and it fulfilled its contract. The same with many other civilizations that have come and gone, and you have distant writings of them that seem to be just stories.

You have been all things, and much more than what you now remember. You are vaster, more powerful, greater than you know yourself to be, and this is what you are walking into in consciousness now. You are walking into an expanded consciousness called fifth dimensional energy, and you will go on from that energy as you desire to know more and more expansion. It will spread to the collective consciousness. It will spread to the place where you will know truly how to live in love, in expansion, moment by moment by moment.

Separated ego will be a story. It will have played its part and you will thank it for being part of the scripting of the staging that you have done, but you will say to it, "Your contract is finished. I don't need you anymore. I remember Oneness with my creative divinity. Now what can I create?"

And because you will be in a state of love, you will create more and more love, because love is expansive. When you have fallen in love with someone, you have forgotten small self. You have been so caught up in love of another one or a beloved pet that you have expanded into a place of Oneness with them, and it has felt wonderful.

When you were young and foolish and you did not know any better (smile), you fell in love, and some of you have stayed there. Most of you have been called back into the world and you have put limitations around the love, but it is always with you, and any time you want to remember love, you can.

Any time you want to know love, call upon me, for I love you with a love that is undying and unchanging. I am your lover. Always I am with you. So if you want to know love and you feel that there is not much love in the world, call upon me. I will not forsake you. I have never forsaken you.

Even during the crucifixion when it seemingly was the end of me, what did I do? I came back. Never will I leave you. Lo, I am with you always. No matter where you move to, no matter where you journey, no matter how bad things seem to be or how good, always I am with you.

The collective consciousness now is calling for that kind of love. It is calling out, it is seeking in books, in your movies, in the magnetic recordings, in your groupings. The collective consciousness wants to know the next stage of being, and so you are going to usher it in, in a process of ascension, an ascension in consciousness.

The energy that you are has been from before time began, and after the purpose of time has been fulfilled, you will still be. That is how powerful you are. That is how great you are. So allow yourself every time there is a feeling of questioning, of wondering where to go, what to do, take the deep breath and say to yourself, "I am loved," because you are. And then take it one step further: "I Am Love," because that is truly what you are.

You are the expansiveness of love. I use the word "love" because it is the closest concept to knowing the divinity of you. When you feel in love, when you feel loved, that allows a crack in the door, the window opens a little way, and you have a glimpse of the vastness, the expansiveness that you are, the peace that you are. Have the intent to abide in the divinity of love which you are. Have the intent. Set that for yourself every morning when you first awaken and you take that first yawn. As you take that first yawn, allow yourself to feel expansive. Take in all of the air around you and know that you are filling up the energy of being with the love that you are, and you are so excited to go out that day and share it with everyone. Allow your love to encircle the globe. Visualize it.

You will remember. You will read stories that excite you. You will read intellectual concepts that excite you. You will use the mind to serve the heart. The heart wants to love, to take in everyone as One—capital "O". And so you will use your mind, the intellectual capacity that is coming very rapidly now with all of your technology, to prove to yourself that you are connected.

The awakening consciousness—that is where you stand. It is the process of ascension in consciousness, of being in peace, being in love, knowing the divinity that activates everything; being the Beholder that stands back and knows, proclaims the Oneness, the true Oneness of everything that is happening. Everything serves the atonement, the realization of at-One-ment.

Allow yourself to have the feet in third dimension yet, because there are worldly things that have to be taken care of. But allow the inner being of you to be at peace, knowing that truly you have fashioned all of the activities around you and you can behold their true meaning.

Allow yourself to live in an ascended consciousness, even while you are doing the worldly things that have to be attended to. Feel the expansion. Feel the love. Abide in love. Abide in non-judgment. And if you must judge, judge from the place of the Beholder that sees everything from the standpoint of w, h, o, l, e—holy—vision. And know that always, as you walk into this space, the holy ascended space, always I am with you.

Fear nothing, for the Christ is guiding you.

The Necessity for Love

Beloved Friend, again Peace be with you. I am the one you have called Joseph, earthly father to Jeshua, and in a later incarnation I have been known as St. Germain.

The Council of One has requested that I speak with you about a topic that is most timely and most important. It is the topic of the necessity for love.

You have been discerning that there are many changes happening in your world; many changes on what you call the political front; many changes where brother is set against brother and sister against sister.

You have many who are finding division within their families, biological and extended, even within their own geo-political groupings as you call them.

You are also finding that our holy Mother Earth is giving you messages all over terra firma. You have ones remarking on the climate conditions, saying, "I have never seen in so many years such dramatic climatic changes happening;" not only in your own area, but all across holy Mother Earth.

Mother nature, Mother Earth is mirroring for you the war that is going on within the grouping and within each individual, in truth, because you have questionings; you have some warring that is going on within yourself as to, "What should I do, where should I go, how should I be, what decisions should I make?"

As you feel it on an individual level, it is also symbolic of the whole, and the whole is showing you quite a demonstration that there is much that is asking for love.

Now, when I speak of love, it is to speak of a Love greater than what you understand human love to be.

Human love is important. Human love allows you to feel the expansiveness where you lose yourself in your feelings and your support for another one, where you become One with another one. You feel so much love that you are with that one as One, and your heart goes out to that one and you give it over to that one in great love, to the place of forgetting for a moment or so, or perhaps even longer, your own individualized self. So human love is very, very important as an indicator of what Love with a capital "L" is.

Love with a capital "L" is the expansiveness of divinity, of the Intelligence—capital "I"—of divinity. There is a necessity right now for Love upon this plane; otherwise, there is going to be what you see as an upheaval, the likes of which you as humans have not seen in a long, long time. You have seen it in other civilizations, other ages long, long time ago, where a civilization has reached a certain peak of technology, of intelligence—lower case "i"—and of development, and then has collapsed.

You have even in what is known as your linear history—and there is much more history than what has been written about—the great civilizations that have come up because there has been a vision, an idea that has been within many as a whole, of respect for all life. And then, as the human tendency of divisiveness has come into it, there has been judgment and separation, ego, greed, and temporal power which has then brought the civilization into a *de*volvement.

You are standing now at a place where you have a civilization which is birthing itself, hopefully, into a greater world civilization; not without birthing pains, as you have seen. And it has yet to be seen whether this vision will become a reality upon this plane and whether the civilization as you know it now—this geo-political grouping and other groupings on the face of terra firma—may come to a place of great respect one for another with allowance and love, or there may be the divisiveness and fear that destroys the vision that many have had, the vision which has allowed the civilization to grow as it has for some time.

It is important that you begin with what you understand love to be. Begin with something that is easy for you to love: perhaps the four-footed ones; perhaps a mate; perhaps a good friend who has always been there for you; someone or something that you can feel an expansiveness of the heart with and for.

Now, as I speak, all of you have a vision of something or someone that you love, or it may be a vocation, a career, a creative venue that you have, where you love it, you lose yourself in it, you lose the identity of small self in it. Start with that premise first, because that you do know. You know how to love.

All of you have been in love at one time or another with something or someone, and you know the feeling. Start with that first. Honor it. Feel it. Practice it. Maybe it has been a long time ago; maybe it has not been a long time ago. But even if it has seemingly, in linear time, been a long time ago, you can still pull it up in memory. You are as a computer; you can bring it up in memory, and you can live in that space of love and the space of expansiveness which allows the small self to be loved for a moment or so in the expansiveness.

Then allow that to spread to all of the brothers and sisters with whom you have discourse, all of the ones you work with—begin to see them in love. Already, I know that you try to do that. Allow yourself to expand that even further and to feel yourself able to look at another one and say, either with the words or definitely with the eyes, "I know that which you are, and I love that which you are, because you are Love itself."

As you will do that with everyone you meet in every day, you will find yourself living in a bubble of love, because you are giving it out, and as you give it out, it has to flow through you, so you are in that space the whole time.

This is most important to remember, especially if you are going through any kind of relationship that seems to be a bit challenging. Allow yourself to feel the love going out to everyone you meet.

Be so caught up in that love that there is not space for feeling a lack of love. Feel yourself in a bubble of love, because truly that *is* what you are. And as you will consciously live in that space and consciously speak to other ones how much you appreciate them, how happy you are that they are on this journey with you, you will feel yourself in the bubble of love.

Your economics are another indicator mirroring to you the unsteadiness of ones wanting to live in love, and yet feeling divided. And so your economics and your financial transactions are going up and down. They are indicators which show you that the collective consciousness, of which you are a part, is wavering; it wants to find solid love and be in the space of love, and yet it is often pulled out of it into a world view that sees duality, that sees divisiveness, that sees from the place of fear rather than love.

That is why the Council of One wants me to speak very strongly with you about the necessity for love, rather than living from the space of fear. Because if you are not living in love, you are living from a place of fear, a fear that there could be lack, that something could be missing, whether it be a relationship, whether it be the monetary concerns, whether it be anything you can or cannot name.

Give unto yourself love instead of fear. You do not need it from other ones. In truth, they cannot give it to you. You have to claim it yourself. That goes for everything that you feel comes from outside or must come from outside of yourself. It cannot come from outside of yourself. It has to come from within. The reason it has to come from within is because that is where it abides. It abides within you. Everything that you would seek is within you.

The love that we speak of, the human love: that is within you. The memory of human love: that is within you.

The love that you allow to flow out to others: it is within you. And the love as Intelligence and divinity that is within you from before time began, before you even thought to bring forth form, bodies, human experience; before you thought to bring that reality into being: that is within you. You are Intelligence—capital "I"—and divine.

Then when you have gone past the place of extending the love to the ones you can see, bring to mind the brothers and sisters that you do not see with the physical eyes, the ones that perhaps you hear about with your news media, the ones perhaps that you read about in your newspapers, the ones perhaps that you read about or see pictures of on your most wonderful web, the Internet, where you find that you are interconnected with everyone—it is great proof of the Oneness of you—and love them.

There are many in this world right now who are living from a place of fear; living from a place of anger; feeling that they have been disrespected, disowned, displaced; "dissed," in others words. Allow yourself to extend to them inclusion and love. Any time they come to mind, include them, and say to them mentally, "You are my brother, you are my sister"—because they are—"I include you in my bubble of love."

You are most powerful. Oftentimes the world speaks to you that you are nothing more than just the body and that you are nothing more than just the personality, and even that is not great. That is the way the world speaks to you, but that is not the truth of your being. The truth of your being is that you are all interconnected, all divine, having a human experience, *and you are all in this together.*

As you will recognize love within yourself—that is why we started with loving yourself—you will extend it to others, and you will know the truth of that love as it goes out from you to the other ones who are in the mind's eye, or as your news media will show them to you. Include them in your family of love.

There have been, as you have seen in linear history, many generations who have lived in separation one from another, where each new generation has grown up thinking that they have to defend themselves, they have to defend their territory, they have to defend their belief, because they feel that what they believe in and what they stand for is going to be overtaken and destroyed by others, as it has been in many histories.

You are now at a most pivotal place. You, the ones who are of like mind, are at a pivotal place of power; not as the world defines power, but a pivotal place where you can influence the course of history. Take that to heart. Live from the space of the heart. Live it consciously.

As much as you are able, allow any petty concerns about your own life, your own family, whatever small challenges you may be having, to be set aside. Because truly, if you measure all of the small challenges, all of the little things that come up in a day—and I know that they do—if you measure those against the good of humankind in all of history going forward from this point, you will see that those little challenges, those things that seem so big when you are right in the middle of them, are but passing and temporal and do not mean anything more than dust.

If you feel you want to change something and you are living in the space of saying, "I want to, I want to believe, I want to really know, I want to really feel that I have the power to influence collective consciousness," allow yourself to know the power of the breath, because each and every one of you—and within the mind's eye as you bring to mind all of the loved ones and everyone that you can imagine in your news media family—is breathing the breath of life.

So take what you hold deep in your heart—love. Take it; put the hands in front of you in an "L"shape, right hand parallel to the chest, left hand supporting the right hand at the wrist and extended outward, and think to yourself, "I take the love of my heart and I place it in an outgoing position, in a direction which is sent out to the collective consciousness." If you want to give it a bit more power, blow with the breath of love of your heart in the direction the left hand is pointing and extend it to the rest of the world.

The Council of One is most adamant that you become aware in this moment and from this time on of your power; that you are not powerless; that you are not just living an individual life. You have individual concerns, but you are much more than that.

Right now is the time for you to make a choice: where will you abide? Will you abide in the world that yet lives from fear, or will you live from the place of divine love that says, "I am the power of Love from before time began. I am Intelligence, divine Intelligence, and I send it forth. It is my conscious choice to send it forth, and forth it goes."

You stand now at a most important place in history. It is difficult to see the forest for the trees. When you are in the middle of the forest, and as you are in the middle of human life, it is difficult to see sometimes the whole. But you can do it, and it is most necessary that those of you who have the ears to hear and the heart which will open, that you act consciously now; not five years from now; not when you get a degree in metaphysics; not when everything in your life comes together perfectly—because in truth everything is already perfect in your life; it takes only the shift in the perception to see it perfectly.

The time is now. I have delivered the message. Take you the message to heart. Use the symbolism that I have shown you of the upright right hand and the left hand extended outward, making what you call the right angle; the right hand symbolizing the heart, the love; the left hand symbolizing the direction that you are sending the love out. And then with your power of conscious breath, blow that love out to everyone and see it going out to everyone.

You can, you will, and I charge you with the directive to change the direction of human life in this time.

—*Joseph/St.Germain*

Memories

Beloved one, memory is a most wonderful aspect which you have built into the human experience. You can remember experiences of past lifetimes, the present lifetime, and, as you can imagine, experiences of future lifetimes. You can remember experiences which you had as a small one; some experiences which were very nurturing, very loving, where you knew the parent would always take you in their arms and make everything better for you. And, you have memories of times when the one that you trusted was not always there for you; in fact, did not understand you and was not there in the way that you wanted them to be there for you.

So you have a variety of memories, memories which can now be seen in a new light because you are a new person with new understanding. Now you can go back and you can forgive when necessary, and as we have explained other times, the meaning of "forgive" is to "give love for" in place of—to give love in place of what has seemed to be harsh judgment, resentment, guilt, shame; to give love to yourself in the situation that you remember and to give love to the other one who was involved in the situation.

You are not now the small person who needed, seemingly, the parent's protection. You are in a new place as a new person, because you have come through many experiences. You are not the person that you used to be. You are not the same as you were several sentences ago. There has been revelation, something which has clicked within you as we have been speaking. I work with you with the words, with the concepts, with the ideas that trigger the remembrance of Truth within you, but I also work with you energetically at a deeper level so that there is much of healing which happens.

You have memories of past lifetimes, some of which have been happy, some of which have been most noble, some of which have been most fulfilling. They are in your memory bank, and you call upon them sometimes; they are there for you. You have memories of other past lifetimes where you have had challenges, and you have brought those memories with you, stored in the body as cell memory, the same as the good memories—as you will judge good and bad. They come with you.

You bring all of those memories with you as a huge treasure chest to any experience you have in this lifetime. That is why I say unto you so often to breathe, because when you take that deep breath and you allow the space of peace, what you are doing is accessing the memory bank. You are accessing all of the memories that pertain to whatever you have been struggling with, looking at, thinking about, contemplating, and you get to choose from the memory bank that which will serve you in any particular experience.

The creative Isness of you is never static. It is forever expressing and experiencing and expanding. In some of your memories you have had memory of ones abandoning you, leaving you, maybe through releasing the body. And you understood that it was their choice to release the body. The mind said, "I understand that that's how it has to be, but I miss you." Now, this reality says that there is separation, but in truth, there is not separation. Anyone you have ever loved is always a part of you, and the memory of that one can be seen in wholeness, even if experiences at the time were seen through the worldly eyes to be tragic and challenging.

You can go back to those memories and you can say to that one, "I am not the person that I was when we were in that relationship." You listen for half a second—and I suggest strongly that you listen for half a second—to what they will say to you, because they are going to be saying to you, "I am not the person that I was then. I have changed also because of the experiences we shared together and because of new perspectives since then."

You are as teachers for each other. You come together in the most wonderful relationships and you sandpaper—oh, you sandpaper—and sometimes it gets so hot, you make a smoother person of each other, to the place where you can get rid of the debris and you can get down to the love.

That is what human life and other life expressions are about: coming to the place of the awareness of the wholeness of you. That is why you call to yourself the experiences in relationships that may seem at the time not to be what you want, but they do a most wonderful job of sandpapering.

I have spoken to you many times about how when one chapter finishes, separated ego resists change. Then, after a while, you move into the next chapter and you look back at the old chapter and you can say, "Oh, I'm glad I'm not in that old chapter any longer. I am beginning to like this new chapter. I like the feeling of knowing my own strength, the feeling of knowing I have friends that I didn't know I had, the feeling of knowing that I *can* make my way."

Sometimes as you work your way through the chapters of the book of life, that one who called you worthless in chapter two, by the time you get to chapter fifteen, comes back to you and says, "I didn't realize what we had together. You're not worthless at all. I kind of like you. In fact, I thank you for the time we had together." And then you can say, "This is good, because if you hadn't kicked me out of chapter two into chapter three, I wouldn't have known chapters three, four, five, and all the other chapters and all of the good things that I have experienced since then."

All of you have memory which serves you very well: memory of past lifetimes; memory of what has happened in this lifetime where you have "learned" what allows you to feel good about yourself and good about others. You go to that memory bank and you access—like you would do on a computer—the memory bank of, "Have I ever lived this situation before? What happened in situations like this before? What can I draw on that will help me in this present situation? How can I see this in a different way? Have there been lifetimes where I have lived a relationship like this or an experience like this where I knew love and it was okay?"

I highly, strongly suggest to you that you go back to the memory bank and remember the good experiences. You are very, very adept at bringing out the bad experiences. You have those right there at your fingertips in the memory bank. They come up first: times when you have suffered, times when you have had the tragedies, the abandonment, the loss, times when you have seemingly made a mistake. Those come up very quickly, but I highly, strongly suggest to you that you take the deep breath and you access the memory bank and consciously call forth the good memories: how it feels to be loved, how it feels to be taken care of, how it feels to trust yourself, how to know that always you are held in the everlasting arms of Love itself.

You may have to dig a bit. You may have to consciously think about good memories, because many of you have come through challenging times in this lifetime, and those are the memories that are going to come up first. But allow yourself perhaps another deep breath and say, "Okay, I don't want first, second, third, fourth choice. I want to go to another page." You go to your computer-mind and you type in, "Good memories," and bring them up to where you can remember in the feeling nature how it *feels* to be right, to be okay, to be courageous, to be loved. The Truth is that always you *are* okay. You *are* loved. You *are*—even in the world of judgment—right.

As I have said, you make no wrong decisions ever. You make choices, and you live with the effects of the choices, but they are not wrong choices. You do not make wrong choices. So click on all the choices that you have and Behold them. Click on the good ones and bring those up and feel them. Get right into the middle of the feeling of how it feels to have a sanctuary or a place where there are friends who love you.

Separated ego loves to give you opportunity to be buffeted about by the opinions of the world, of the friends, of the brothers and sisters, of the co-workers, of the boss, of the mates. They will be very quick to give you their assessment. But that is their assessment from their perspective, and they do not walk in your sandals. They do not know your past lifetimes. They do not know; they cannot know what you have experienced even in this lifetime up to this point. The only person who knows that is you, and you carry that as memory.

As I have said, usually what comes up first in the memory bank are all of the things that feel wrong, that feel that you have made a mistake, and that something needs to be corrected. "If only…." I hear that so often in the prayers as people will pray to me. "Jeshua, if only you could change this for me. If only I had known. If only…."

Well, I say to you, there has never been a wrong decision, so that you do not have to go back and "if only" it. But you do have the opportunity to change your perspective about anything by stepping back into the place of the Beholder and beholding it anew.

Look at the silver platter that separated ego shows you. What do you want to choose from that platter? Choose the sunshine, the Light, the love of life itself. Choose you this day what serves you in remembering your divinity. Memories are a most important tool if they are used wisely. Do not beat yourself up with old memories of abandonment, of judgment, of wrong choices, a whole laundry list of things that you would have done differently IF. Do not dwell on what seems to be wrong.

Search a little bit further for the goodness of you: the memories of times when you have been hugged by another one and totally loved and accepted for just who you are; when it did not matter whether the hair was one of the bedheads; when it did not matter whether you had the fat thighs or the thin thighs; when it did not matter whether you were scrawny or abundant. None of that mattered because the person saw past appearances and said, "I love you because you bring out the best in me. I love you because I see the Christ in you, and seeing the Christ in you, I behold the Christ of me."

Now, they may not put it into those words, but that is how the feeling comes through. When you are with the one who totally loves and accepts you just as you are, you can let down the guard. You can let down all of the "shoulds", the appearances. You can even let the belly be as fat as it wants to be. You can just allow yourself to *be*.

That is why when you are with friends who totally accept you as you are, you feel at peace. You can just be yourSelf—capital "S"—and the more you do that, the more love you put into the world, because it starts with you. It starts with you accepting yourself for who you are, fat thighs and all, spirituality and all. It starts with loving yourself and knowing yourself truly from the inside out. As you do that, you put more and more love into the world. You put more and more compassion into the world.

We have spoken other times of compassion; compassion meaning "with passion." Meaning that you are with that other one in their passion, their passion for life. You are with them *as* One. That is what compassion truly means: "I am One with you."

When you are One with another person, you are not going to start beating them up, either physically or emotionally. When you are One with another person, you are in Love with them –capital "L". You are in the place of compassion, which sees another one as yourself and you know yourself to be True. You are the ones who can do it, because you believe in Love. You believe in the power of peace. You believe in the power of divine extension of Life itself, you believe that every life is important and that it is valued. Life can never be extinguished. It is energy and it can never be extinguished. It can be changed into another form, but it can never be extinguished.

Compassion. Go back into your memory bank. When was the last time you felt compassion with someone, either two-footed or four-footed? Sometimes it is easier to have a memory of unconditional love with the four-footed ones, where you feel completely One in their passion for life, in the simplicity of life. You have all known the feeling of being One with another one, whether two-footed or four-footed. There have been times in your life when you have felt so One with another expression of life that you felt whole. Remember that feeling. Take it with you into the workplace, into the world, into all of your interchanges with brothers and sisters. You will change yourself. And more than that, you will change your world.

If your leaders would breathe with each other before they make decisions, there would be more compassion. If you in your dealing with the co-workers and the friends will breathe and allow yourself the place of peace which accesses the memory bank of how compassion feels, how good it feels when you know that you are valued, there would be more love and understanding in the world.

Allow yourself now to take a deep breath. Feel yourself so loved; truly you are worthy, worthy of great, great love and compassion. You are strong. You are courageous. You are able to make decisions which allow your life to go forward in a healthy, wholesome way. You never walk the path alone. Always I am with you.

You Are the Power of Now

Beloved one, take a deep breath and feel yourself surrounded by the golden white light which is called the aura, and with another deep breath, feel yourself taking that golden white light into the body, in through the crown chakra, down throughout all of the body, down to the fingertips and down to the toes, allowing all of the cells of the body to come alight again, feeling expanded in their Light. Then taking another easy breath, feel yourself centered in the heart; feel yourself centered in a place of peace. Know that you are loved beyond all understanding, and that you *are* love itself. Feel yourself expansive in that love, in the healing, nurturing love. Know yourself to be a space of sacred peace.

Now, some time ago I spoke with you that you are the power of the future, that you are the one envisioning the future, and that the future does not exist except as you will mold it and shape it and envision it. You are the power of the future, and it will be as you decree it. The future has not been made yet.

Then I have heard you thinking, and as you took it a little further, you said, "Well, if the future comes out of my visioning, where is the future right now?" The future, as you have discerned, is right now. As you make it, you are living the future already. So you are, in essence, the power of Now, projecting it into the future as you understand linear time to be.

You are the power of Now. There is truly no other time except Now, and even as you will envision your future as you want it to be, you are envisioning it right now.

There is nobody "out there" orchestrating what your life has to be, although there *are* ones who will say that they are directing that you to have to be to work at a certain time, that you have to get a load of paperwork done before you are allowed to leave the desk, or that you have to make so many golden coins in a certain timeframe, otherwise they will replace you and put someone else in your place.

There may be ones who are saying that they have power over you, but in truth, you are momentarily giving them the power to say that to you, and if you do not accept their suggestion of power, what they say does not mean a thing, because you know who is in charge. You know who is having the power or giving the power to them momentarily. Yes, there are certain things in the world to render unto Caesar, but you will understand that you are the power that even brings Caesar into existence.

You can take your understanding of the power that you are and see what you want the next day to be. If you are dealing with a problem of the body, of healing, and you have been told that such and such is true, that is all it is: you have been told that such and such is true.

Do you know it to be true? Not really. Maybe it is not true. "Maybe I am whole and perfect." That feels good. "Maybe I don't have to carry all of the stress and strain. Maybe it was only my imagination anyway, and I can let it go." That feels good.

"Maybe relationships are just a way of giving me opportunity to love; to love another person as they are calling out for love, and to love myself; to know my own divinity, my own wholeness, and to know that I don't need another person to make me whole.

"I *want* another person, because I want someone to receive my love. I want them to be there, and I want to see the change on their face as they understand that I really, really love them." But you know what? You can do that without them being present. You can bring them up in the mind's eye, whether they be incarnate, or maybe they have passed on, or maybe you have never seen them in the physical, but you can bring them up in the mind's eye and you can say, "I love you. I love you so much that I am filled with love, and I see you as radiant light."

Because truly that is what everyone, every individuated extension of the Father/Mother/Creator is. "I see you as radiant love, and that fills *me* with love. It has to fill me with love, because that's the space I'm in when I'm saying to another one, 'I love you. I love you so much that I can love myself loving you.'"

Try that one on for size. "I love you so much that I can love myself for loving you." The world does not teach you that. The world teaches you separation. The world teaches you give and take; that you must give, others must take. Others often *will* take, even if you do not want to give, but the truth of it is, no one can ever keep you from loving. That is your choice, and you can love them so much that you can love yourself because you are loving them, and that feels very good and freeing.

It begins to allow the water of life to flow again, and it begins to allow a change even in the outer, for the outer is only a picture of the inner. What you envision in the inner, what you truly feel in the inner, is going to out-picture. That is why you have had so many messages from our holy Mother, the Earth, calling for attention; saying, "Pay attention." Why is there an earthquake? It is because ones in the collective consciousness have felt an upheaval within themselves. Sometimes an upheaval has been good, because there needed to be a bit of reshuffling, and earthquakes are good at that: reshuffling; allowing people again to become clear about their priorities.

Pay attention to what is going on inside. Claim your power to heal; to awaken in the morning and to say, "I am free to choose in this day whom I will serve. I am free to choose where I will go, what I will do; I am free."

If you would take that to heart, you would see such a change, and you *will* see such a change, because it is going to happen. When you will take it to heart, that "*I am free* to be that which I am; I am totally free to be the divine holy extension of the one Creator; I am totally and completely free to *be*, just to *be*," all of the shackles of the world fall off.

No longer do you need certain pieces to fall into place to make you happy. No longer do you need a relationship that is perfect to make you happy. No longer do you have to have the body that is going to speak to you that it is all in great shape and you do not have any aches and pains.

You *won't* have any aches and pains, because you are free, totally and completely free in the power of the Now, the power of the moment, to know that you are free, totally free.

What is age? It is only a thinking in the mind. All of you have felt from time to time as young as little children. You have been so happy, so turned on by something that happened that you have said, "Hey, I feel really young. I feel really, really good. I don't know what it is, but today I feel just really, really great. My eyes sparkle. I feel truly alive. I am young once again. All of the aches and pains and the things I was dreading, all have become no-things."

You are free. In this moment you are free to be that which you are. You are so loved. I can never tell you enough, over and over and over, how loved you are. You are love itself. Accept it for yourself. *Feel it* for yourself. Know that you are that love. You are that which you seek. You *are* the love of the Father.

Furthermore, all of you are *starved* for touch. *All* of you want to be touched. That is why you give the hugs. Reach out and touch. Each and every one of you *want* to be touched. You *want* to be held. You *want* to have the nurturing which was there in the beginning. Why is it that the small Child within you calls out? It is to be held once again and nurtured as you were as the incarnate infant; to be held and to be loved. It is to know how you have been held and nurtured by the Love of the Father/Mother from before time began.

It is okay to want that. It is okay even to speak the words to ask of another one, "Please hold me. Please touch me. Please be with me."

You are so loved.

You have the saying in your Scriptures that *God so loved the world that he gave his only begotten Son.* **Who** is the only begotten Son? *You* are. Each and every one of you come forth into this realm, this reality, to bring *life* and *Light* and *love* to this reality. For God, the one Creator, loved the world in all of its chaos and all of its complexity so much that It gave Its only begotten *Self* that ones might know life once again.

You are so loved, every one of you. Play with the imagination: how it feels to be loved and to be at ease. You know so little of at-easement. You know dis-easement all around you, but do you know ease, how it feels to be easy, peaceful? Mmmm, right now you do; you took that deep breath. That is how it feels to be at ease. That is how it feels to be powerful in the Now, to understand the true power—not as the world speaks of power; that is temporal and passing and has many responsibilities and many untruths attached to it—but the true power of being and the true power of freedom and the true power of saying, "I can make this life as I want it to be, and for as long as I want it to be."

Know you that the human being is the only species in your reality that worries about dis-easement, dying? For the most part, ones dread dying, releasing the body. Others—other species in this reality—live in the Now. Have you observed your four-footed ones recently, the ones known as the dogs, the cats, the alpacas? Where do they live? *When* do they live? Now.

They do not worry about "what that other dog said to me yesterday." They just live in the Now. They do not worry about what the morrow is going to bring. It is not even in their reality to think of it.

How about the lilies of the field? They certainly do not worry about, "Is there going to be sunshine? Is there going to be rain?" They just *do* what they are: to grow; to be life. The same with your trees. Trees do not know death. Trees do not worry abut dying. Trees live…well, truly, the energy lives on forever, but a tree in its form lives until someone cuts it down. And certainly, after it is cut down, it does not worry about, "Oh, my goodness, I've been cut down and I'm in pieces." It still is energy. It knows itself to *be* energy; to be; as you are; just to be; the energy of life, extending Itself in whatever form is chosen at the time.

The power of Now; right now. The deep breath. Live you always in the Now, for that *is* the truth of your being. You are the makers of time. Live you always in the Now. Live you always in ease, with the deep breath, knowing your wholeness, knowing how loved you are, for in truth, you *are* the love that you seek. Now.

The Hologram of Now

Beloved one, we come now to the essence of the power of the Now. You have heard it said many times that you make your own reality—lower case "r"—and how you live within that reality and how you are not separate from your reality. I would use an example shown in one of your science fiction movies, the one known as "Star Wars," where there was shown to be the hologram of a sword fight, and ones in the movie were watching the sword fight as it would be right in front of them. Do you remember that one?

This is truly a good example of what you are doing. You are making a much larger hologram, inviting all of the ones to be in your hologram to play with each other, or not, and you are watching what is going on. You have invited everyone to be part of what you are experiencing. And often separated ego will run onstage and say, "Well, if you are creating this hologram and you see that there is warring going on between brother and brother and sister and sister, you must be doing something wrong. You are guilty of bringing what you call the negative into the picture."

But in truth, when you stand back from it and you are in the place of Beholder, you watch how even the most seeming horrendous acts bring forth awakenings with the people who are involved in those acts and also with ones who are watching what is happening, having it brought to them on the television screen via your news media, sometimes feeling your heart open for the ones who are enacting these parts.

There is much more that is going on beyond the appearance, and there is much opportunity for love and awakening. Oftentimes an experience that seems to be most horrendous allows ones to see and feel compassion, sympathy, understanding, where the heart opens and there is Oneness with the person or persons going through an experience, so that you feel you are walking in their sandals.

Truly, you *have* walked in their sandals. You have experienced warfare, conflict, challenge; otherwise, there would not be the computer card in your computer that registers and says, "Yes, I understand this." You *have* lived those lifetimes to the place where you now understand how it feels to be in such a situation, and your heart does open, and you reach out in worldly ways that are tangible to help ones with the golden coins or with your gifts of different kinds.

If ones come to your doorstep, if they are neighbors and they need something, your heart opens and you share with them what you have. With ones who may be a bit farther away, you send whatever you can send; in other words, you do as your guidance tells you. But in that moment there is a knowing of Oneness, a knowing that that brother/sister is walking in sandals "that I have walked in in other lifetimes; otherwise, I would not recognize it, I would not know what they are going through."

And so it brings in you a knowing of Oneness. Everything—as I say to you over and over—leads to the realization of Oneness. Every happening, no matter how it looks, has in it the potential for awakening and realizing that you are One with each other. You understand feelings. You understand journeys. You understand each other because you have been there, no matter what one is going through. And your heart opens to support the other ones on their journey.

That is the message that I gave to you two thousand years ago, that truly you *are* your brother. Everything is within your consciousness—everything that you see, everything that you experience, everything that you see others experiencing and you understand that what they are going through is within your consciousness.

There is truly only One of us having the experience that the One is expressing as many. That is who and what you are. You are the One expressing as the many. If you remember nothing else from this message, remember that the experience that you are having is within your consciousness, and you are the One expressing as the many.

That which you would seek, you can out-picture in your consciousness. You are that powerful. We have talked about this many, many times as to how powerful you are, so powerful, so creative that you can bring your point of consciousness to the place where you say, "I am a body; I am a personality separate from others. I have talents that are separate from others. I drive a different vehicle than others do. I have different challenges, different family, different generational teaching than others do."

Separated ego loves to support that script. However, as the energy, the infinite energy of Oneness, you *allow* yourself—lower case "s"—to experience yourself as separate. But in Truth, you are not.

You have tested this as you have been coming through life and you have found something that you love or someone that you love, and you lose yourself in that love. You only see the loved object, whether it be another person or whether it be a beloved pet or even an occupation, and you feel the unconditional expansive love which for a moment or so does not recognize separation.

You know that you are the same energy, and you love that one or that expression of self so much that you lose the limitations of who you have thought yourself to be, and you are in joy, divine joy.

Now, if there are things in your hologram that you want to shape-shift, you can do that. You work with allowing, first looking at what there is in the hologram as you understand your life to be, and then allowing everything to be seen as good. You have that saying in your holy Scriptures, that God—you—made everything, and on the seventh day—in other words, the last finished day—you looked at everything and you called it good. You have forgotten that part.

You now look at things and it is habitual—but if it is a habit, it can be changed — to look for what is wrong. You have been taught by generational teaching to look for what could be made better, what is wrong, even a small thing that could be perfected a bit. It is already perfect, but you have been taught by generational teaching—the parents, the grandparents, the ancestors have said, "Life is imperfect," and you as the small one have said, "Well, they have lived more years than I have; they must know," and so you have bought the message that was given to them down through the generations.

Seeds have been planted a long time ago, even before this lifetime, and those seeds of desire to know harmony and to know Oneness are growing. They are as little seedlings growing, becoming stronger, becoming more part of your awareness, and you work with this from time to time as an idea comes to you and you wonder sometimes, "Where did that idea come from?" Well, it comes from the little seedling that was planted maybe many lifetimes ago of wanting to awaken to the place of divinity, the place that knows Oneness with All, the place that says, "I am okay," because you are, "and I want to feel that. I will start with acknowledging that for myself."

It has been habitual training to look outside of yourself to separated, individuated energy and to ask for the validation from others. "If others see my worth and they mirror it back to me and they say how wonderful I am, then I must be okay. But if they don't recognize the angel that I am, the Light that I am, the little Child—capital "C"—that I am, then I must not be worthy." It has been generational teaching for a long, long time to look outside, seemingly, because there is nothing really outside of yourself, but to look to others for the validation.

So start with validating yourself. First thing in the morning when you wake up and you take that deep breath, know that truly you are a work of wonder that allows that deep breath to energize the body. Recognize the miracle that you are doing in that moment of focusing upon the form of energy that you have brought together called a body. Recognize the miracle that was not there a moment before that. You *are* a wondrous being, that you can bring together this hologram and call it real.

Now, your Reality—capital "R"—is what allows you to use the energy to make your reality—lower case "r"—and to feel that that reality is true. But your true Reality is divine.

Your world is coming to a place where it is no longer being able to be so separate, one country from another. You have a global understanding. Your news media has seen to that. And your internet, your worldwide web is very good at keeping you connected with ones who you may never see with the physical eyes, but you know what is happening with them.

You have an understanding at this point that looks like everything is in chaos. Some of it is going through upheaval, and will continue to go through some upheaval, because you have wanted to know global harmony. And so, therefore, your hologram, as you are making it, says, "Well, we have to have some ingredients in here of change. If it is not global harmony right now,"—and it is not, as it appears—"we need to have some change."

And so in the hologram that you are putting forth moment by moment with your consciousness, there is upheaval. But upheaval—as we have said to you many, many times—is good. It is necessary. For when you go out to till the soil, to make something as the garden or the farm crops, the first thing you do is to till the soil.

You are the creative One, seemingly expressing as the many, who is creating moment by moment that which you experience in your consciousness. Take that deeply within the consciousness. *You are the creative One, seemingly expressing as the many, who is creating moment by moment that which you experience in your consciousness.*

You have done this many, many, as you understand lifetimes to be, so many times that separated ego says,

"Well, you have evidence that whatever you try to change for the better won't work." But where is that "evidence"? The "evidence" resides in memory, in an old computer program which, in truth, is outdated; it will not work in your computer any longer.

You have actual computer programs that are like that. They served you well for awhile, and then you got a new computer or you upgraded the computer, and what happened? The old program would not run. Well, that is where you are now with the hologram that you are living. Some of those old programs do not run any longer.

That which seemingly happened to you a long time ago in this lifetime or even yesterday, where does it exist? Truly, nowhere; only in memory as you bring it up and you try to relive it. But it is not real. It is no longer real. And you, as the creative master that you are, can say unto it, "Be gone. I don't want you in my memory. You're an old program that does not serve me. I'm going to replace you with an upgrade."

As the creative One that you are, you can change anything and everything in the hologram that you are living *if* you have the will and the determination to breathe and to say, "I am determined to see things differently. Hey, you know, life is really fun. I have a lot of friends. My group of friends has been growing and expanding, and I really feel good about that. I thought I only had maybe one or two friends, but you know, everywhere I go, I make a friend. I see them as a friend, and then they *are* a friend. I have lots of friends, and I'm not afraid to go to a new place and make another friend. It is a talent that I have."

As you will see another one as being a friend in your hologram, that is what they are, what they have to be. That is how powerful you are as the creative master. You smile. Sometimes they smile back right away. Sometimes they look at you questioningly, like, "What's going on?" but it is okay. You have smiled. You have put Light into your hologram.

You have lived the lifetimes of dark holograms, enough that you know those programs. But they are not with you any longer, those programs, and they serve you no longer. You do not need them. You have upgraded, and you are leaving them behind. They no longer exist for you, except as you bring them into the Now reality. So you do not have to have them as companions in your hologram.

If you will understand this concept and really take it to heart; not just mentally, but really take the message to heart — that what you are living is a hologram of your making — you will begin to understand Oneness. If you will take it to heart and really feel Oneness with everyone, all of your hologram is going to shift and change; it has to, because you are the one making it. You are the one living in the middle of it.

If you could—and you can—step outside of the hologram for a moment—and this is what I have spoken of as the Beholder—to see the hologram that you are making and how one friend and another friend and another friend and another friend are interacting with you on a certain topic, in a certain way, you would begin to understand not just mentally—mentally is good, it is a good start, it has to start there first because it has been your training to start with the mental first—but then take it to the heart and feel how you are interacting with everyone and how you are part of what you are looking at, you would be in awe of what you are creating; not judgment; do not be in judgment of it.

Separated ego, because of habitual "evidence," is going to say, "Well, this hologram is not really perfect." Separated ego, again, is a program that you no longer need. You are finished with it. Look at the hologram that you are living and call it good, because it is.

Take my message to heart. Examine, as the Beholder, the hologram of what you are putting into your reality—lower case "r". Do not judge, but be in awe of what you have created. Look to the power of Now and behold your hologram, beloved One. There is only One of us, creating, living, experiencing the Now. You are the One.

So be it.

The Parable of the Camel Trader

Beloved one, I would share with you a story. In your holy Scriptures it would be called a parable; it is a story. Once upon a time, as you would understand time to be, a little boy was born into a family that raised animals. They had sheep, they had goats, and they had camels. The father of the family carried on what had been, within the generational lineage, the family business of raising, breeding, and trading camels.

The family was fairly well off, because camels could demand a good price. The family was on a certain caravan route that went to a very busy seaport, and so there was much trade that brought the father much profit.

Over the years, as the father grew older, the family business passed to this little boy, who was now a grown man, and because he was the oldest of the family, he was chosen to carry on the family business of the camel raising, breeding, and trading. It was a good business that he knew. From the very beginning, he saw how it provided for the family, and more than that, he had a fondness for the animals.

He enjoyed being with the sheep. He enjoyed being with the goats. He saw how life was an exchange: the sheep would give the wool for the garment making, and the goats gave their milk and sometimes their meat. The sheep also gave of their meat, and the camels brought in a good price when the caravans came by and needed more camels to carry the burdens of the trade that they were taking to and from the seaport.

As a young boy he had spent most of his days with the animals to the place where he had a common language with them, an instinctive language. There was much that he shared on a level that went deeper than just the words, and there was great love.

As he became a man and took over the family business, he took to himself a wife and began a family of his own. The camel trade proved for them a good livelihood, and he felt very good about being able to provide for his family.

But as is the way of the world, the caravans found a new route to a new seaport, and the new seaport was busier than the old one. And so the caravans started going a new route, not where he was raising his camels, where his family had lived for many generations, and so the business and the golden coins dwindled.

He wondered, and he cursed the new seaport and the new business and the ones who would be attracted to the new seaport. After all, in his thinking, what was wrong with the old seaport? What was wrong with the old trade route that went by his village? He became very bitter; so bitter that his friends did not want to be around him. His brothers and sisters, who were raising their own families nearby, did not want to be with him.

He was very unhappy, so he reached a decision that he would have to take a group of his camels across land to find the new route of the caravans and set up a new business somewhere else. So he said to his family, "I will set out to see where the new route is and I will scc how the trade is, and when I have established a place, I will send for you."

None of his family was happy about this, because they liked living in the village they had known all their lives, and where the father, grandfather, great-grandfather, great-great-grandfather and all the family members, including the cousins and aunts and uncles, had always lived.

So he set out with a group of his camels to see where the new trade route was and to see how business would be. Along the way one evening during the nighttime, robbers came and stole all but three of his camels, so he was left with only three. He became even more embittered. Why had this happened to him? Life had been good up to a certain point. Why had things changed?

He railed against his God, and he railed against the caravans that had changed their route, and he railed against the new seaport, and most of all he railed against the robbers, the thieves who were very good at setting upon a solitary person traveling alone. That is why the caravans traveled in caravans, as protection.

He went on with his three camels to the seaport to have a look at it to see what he could do to set up a new business there, but he found that the land around the seaport was not to his liking. It was too busy. Too many people were living on the outskirts of the seaport, and they were as bad as the robbers on the way. He did not feel happy being there.

His idea had been to set up a new place where he would breed more camels and establish a new business, but he knew that he was not going to be happy there, and it was not a place where he wanted to bring his family. The more he thought about his family and about his village, he knew that he did not want to be in the area of the new seaport.

One evening it came to him that what was most important was his family, the friendships that he had turned his back on, the happiness that he had felt with the sheep, with the goats, and with raising of the camels, the simplicity of life; not the business of the seaport; not the unscrupulous way that they had dealt with him. He had sold two of his camels for much less than what they were worth, and he was left with one old camel. She was very old. That is why no one wanted to buy her. She was too old for breeding and she was too old to do much heavy work. She was his companion.

So he spoke to this camel and he said, "Let us return unto the village. I see now that what I was looking at, what I was chasing after, is not where my treasure lies, but it is with my family and with the village and the villagers that I have known." And with that, his heart opened; the heart that had been closed, tightly armored for a long time as he saw his camel trade dwindling and the caravans no longer coming near his place.

And so with this one very old camel that had been his friend for many, many years and had bred for him many small young camels that he then sold for a good price, with his very old friend he traveled back to the village. He did not know what to expect, because when he had left, everyone was happy to see him go.

But a most miraculous thing happened. His heart had opened. He was in joy with the stars of the night, with the sun in the daytime, with the grass, the fields, the birds. Every little bit of life in every different form he began to see in a new light.

The camel, his companion from the time he was a little boy, spoke to him and pointed out to him the treasures of life itself. And because he had the communion with the camel, his old friend, when he arrived at the village there was a feeling around him that was new, a feeling of appreciation of All That Is.

He did not care if others did not speak to him, but he loved them. And so, of course, they spoke to him, because they could see that there was a smile upon his face, and they welcomed him home. The family was very happy to have him back home again, and he found that there was enough of the goat milk, of the meat, of the wool, and he had left a few of the camels at home, enough that he could start a new breeding program with them, and he gave camels to the rest of the village.

He had come through generational thinking into the family business. He had broken with the family, turned his back, cursed everything that had been near and dear to him, and left. He had gone afar, had everything taken from him except for the old, old camel that was his dear friend, and everything changed for him.

So when he returned to the village, he was no longer the bitter man who had left. He went on to father some more children who loved him dearly. He had great-grandchildren who loved him and villagers who came and spoke to him about, "What is it like out beyond the village?" And he would say, "It is a grand adventure, and if you want to go, go. But if you have everything that is near and dear and important to you right here, then you do not have to travel abroad to find happiness."

So some of them, being adventuresome, set out on their own. But most of them stayed in the village and are there yet to this day, raising their camels and their sheep and their goats and being very happy in the sunshine and in the rain, celebrating the simplicity of life.

Now, if you want to draw from that story any parallels into this day and time, you are free to draw your own conclusions.

Oftentimes two thousand years ago I would sit with you and I would tell very simple stories. Very little was written down in those days. It was not as you had a certain notebook or computer to take with you. You did not even have the papyrus to write on, usually, because you were simple folk.

It was not until much later that my stories were written down; however, they were simple enough, as this one is, that ones remembered them and passed them down generation to generation until finally someone decided they would write them down and they ended up in your holy collection of *biblos*, the Bible. And so you have in this story the parable of the camel trader, not unlike your investment traders of this day.

Now, beloved one, remember first, foremost, and last, how beloved you are; how greatly I love you; how always I travel with you, I laugh with you, I joke with you; I support you. Allow yourself always to look upon the glass that is half full as opposed to half empty, and to count, simple as it sounds, your blessings, for this is a good life.

The Parable of the Widow

Would you like to have another story? Okay, we will have another story.

In your language, a long, long time ago there was a young maiden. She was quite comely, good looking, pretty you would call her, and of good demeanor, happy, so that in her village she had many suitors, young men who were interested in having her spend the rest of the lifetime with them.

Her father looked over the various young men who were interested in marrying this young maiden and he chose for her one who came from a family that had many golden coins. And so the young maiden married this young man, and together they grew to love each other. She gave birth over time to some children: first a boy, and they rejoiced in the boy, and as he grew to be a toddler, there came to be another child in the family, a little girl who very much resembled the young maiden when she was a very young girl.

As that one became a toddler and the boy became a bit older, there came to be another child in the family, another boy, a younger brother, and they rejoiced over the younger brother and it was a very happy family.

And in the fullness of time, there was another child born, another little girl, so that the young maiden, as she grew into womanhood and motherhood, had two boys and two girls, and she rejoiced in the small ones. She rejoiced in what they were learning and what they would share with her, how they would run and play in the sun, how they would run and play in the rain, how they would help tend the cattle and the sheep.

In time, as is the way of the world, news came to their village that there was a warring going on in a neighboring land, and the older son chose to go off to be with some of the other young men to fight for what he saw to be right and to protect his village.

His mother was not happy to see him go, but it was his choice, and so she gave him her blessing, as did the father, and the young man went off and left the family.

The first daughter grew to be a young maiden, again very comely and pretty, resembling her mother when she was a young maiden, and she had suitors, young men in the village who were interested in her. So in time she was married to one of them and moved to a section of land not far away where they built their own dwelling. And in time the mother became a grandmother with great rejoicing.

News came from afar that the older son had perished in a battle and would not be returning, and there was sadness that the mother felt, because her firstborn held a place deep in her heart and she lamented that he was not coming home.

But she had the grandchildren, and the other younger son married and stayed in the next village, and in time there were grandchildren there, and in time the younger daughter also married and had children, so there were quite a few of the grandchildren around her, and she was quite busy with them.

And there came upon the land what you would now call a plague, a sickness, and the older daughter and some of the grandchildren perished in the plague. So there was a sadness and a sense of loss again for the ones she had loved and held in her arms. She could no longer do that with the body, but in her heart she still felt the love.

In time, the beloved husband passed on and released his body and she became a widow, a widow with two of her children and some of the grandchildren still in her life. Then there came the hoards of what would be called the barbarians who overran the land. Her two children and all of the grandchildren were slain before her eyes.

She, being a widow and being very elderly at that point, was spared, in fact ignored. The barbarians did not even see her and did not care. She was too old for them to care about, so she was left in a corner of the dwelling place alone. She began to feel, "What is the use of a life? Where are all the friends, the neighbors, the children, the grandchildren, the husband? Where even are the cattle and the sheep?" for they had been taken by the barbarians who overtook the land.

Everything around had been burned, and she looked out upon the charred land with grief in her heart, because everything she had loved, even down to the blades of grass, seemingly everything had been destroyed and taken from her.

She spent some time rocking herself back and forth in great grief, asking of herself, "Why? Why love, when it is going to be taken away? Why live? Why am I still here?" She held herself, hugged herself with arms around herself, and rocked back and forth, back and forth, and back and forth.

In the rhythm of the rocking she saw herself as the small child that she had been in her mother's arms when she was rocked as a baby, and she felt the love that she had known then. And in the rocking, she felt the rocking that she had done with her own children when they were small, and she felt the love that she had shared with them and how she had rejoiced with them. And she felt, again, the love of each child as it was a babe in arms.

She remembered when they started to grow a bit taller, and she remembered the love they shared with each other as a family. And in the vibration of rocking, in the vibration of remembering love and feeling surrounded by that love, physically surrounded in that love, she came to understand that it was not the loss that was important. It was the love that had been shared that made life worthwhile.

And she came to realize that no barbarian, no stranger, no one could take that love from her. The love that she felt was always hers, was always with her and could not be taken from her. That love was what would always be the value of a life. And with that realization, she drew her last breath and joined her loved ones.

That is known as the parable of the widow, the realization that all that matters in life and all that makes life worth living is love, and that love can never ever be taken from you. Everything else can be taken. Everything else is temporary, but the love that you feel is yours always, and that is what makes life worth living.

Now, beloved one, when the world will present to you its eccentricities, when it will speak to you of vulnerability and that you had better defend yourself, remember the love that you have shared with friends, with family, with ones of like mind. Count yourself blessed by every moment of love, for truly that is where your treasure lies.

Remember the parable of the widow. Remember her realization as she drew her last breath and went happily to join her loved ones, for truly, that will be your story, as well. Your story has a happy ending, for in the last moments what you will remember is the love of loved ones, of family, of friends, of caretakers, whoever is with you, with body or in spirit.

And the next thing you will experience is the light, the light of understanding that, "I am and always will be."

So be it.

The Parable of the Princess in the Castle

Now, beloved one, how about if we have a parable about a princess in a castle? You know what a castle is. You know what royalty is; this is a story about the princess of a royal family.

Once upon a time, before time was, there was a being, a holy being who in its desire to know itself decided to see itself in a mirror, and in looking in the mirror brought forth a belief that there could be two instead of one. Now, it was still one, knowing itself to be two, and we will call this twosome a male and a female, a king and a queen; royalty; holy beings.

They desired to have offspring, to bring forth a child, and so they did. A beautiful princess was born, having all of the qualities of the king and all of the qualities of the queen, because after all, it was one Being experiencing itself as two, and now there were three.

The princess was very much loved, very much adored, admired. The king and the queen wanted to protect the princess to keep her from whatever else there might be, because they knew that there could be creative expression that might be different than the princess.

So the princess grew up knowing that she was greatly loved and protected, and would always be protected. And in time, as they understood time, there was also the prince who was brought forth. And the prince had all of the qualities of the king and the queen, because he was an extension of them.

He looked upon his qualities and he wanted adventure, so in time he left the castle and went out to adventure, to experience, to see what else was out there, but the princess stayed in the castle. The queen and king loved the princess and loved the prince, but, as there was the expression of process, otherwise known as time, they felt the absence of the prince and did not want the princess to leave.

So the princess was well-guarded and kept in the castle where she remains even to this day. The princess looked upon herself to see what qualities she had. She saw how the prince had been enamored with the idea of adventure, but this was not quite what she wanted. She looked inside of herself and discovered that there were qualities there that were of intuition, precognition, love, what you would call now in this day and time the divine feminine.

The divine feminine for a long time now has been kept, guarded in the castle so that no harm would come to her. But this is not what she wanted and, even today, is not what the princess desires. She wants to be known for her qualities, and she wants to come out of the castle to be known for the qualities that are now awakening within many of you.

You have adventured many lifetimes as the prince. You have called forth experiences that allowed within the human realm the adrenaline to rush. You have known and created many examples where you could be the strong masculine.

But the princess, for a long time as you understand process of time, has been kept within the castle and yet very much alive within you, waiting for the drawbridge to be let down. You are now coming to the place where you understand feelings that the world does not understand, knowings that come to you, and you do not know where these knowings come from; visions that come to you, perhaps instantaneous, sometimes longer, sometimes in a long dream as it would be.

You are experiencing intuitive knowing about people, places, happenings. You can move forward in time. You can move in the inner realm to what you would see a future to be, and you can call forth the qualities of the princess and allow her to come out of the castle now to help you make an expanded understanding of the divinity even of the world as the world yet sees itself to be quite chaotic.

You call upon her qualities when you meet a friend and there is the hug that is given, there is the warmth, the smile, the support. She comes rushing forward to meet you. She comes rushing forward to greet another one as you give to them the understanding that, "I know who you are," and you look upon another one and you see the Christ of them, you see the divine being of them.

The princess then is allowed out of the castle. The princess for a long, long, long time as you measure time has been kept hidden away in the castle because the world seemed fit only for the prince, the adventuresome one, the strong one.

Now, the princess is also strong, but her qualities are more gentle, and so she has waited until there would be welcome for her qualities. Now is the time. Allow yourself to invite the princess and the qualities that she embodies, that she symbolizes, to be very much working in your life. Already there have been times when you had to call upon strength that the world did not understand, qualities that the world does not teach and does not value.

That is the princess, the intuitive gentleness, the knowing that goes beyond just the physical or the knowing that goes beyond what *has* been known, into the knowing of the divine Self. So allow the princess to be very much alive in your thought processes. Allow the princess to adventure now with the prince, and understand that both the prince and the princess embody all of the qualities of the One who looked into the mirror and thought that It saw two, and then brought forth the offspring that has seen itself to be separate and different from each other and yet the same, from the same Source.

Jeshua: The Personal Christ
Volume I

Channeled information from Jeshua ben Joseph — Jesus. We hear about reincarnation, channeling, love, Earth changes, ego, the divine feminine, ascension and more. We are reminded of the simplicity and love of Jesus' message to us. Contains a beautiful meditation.

Jeshua walks with us through this book, speaking eloquently on many topics, but none with more passion than on the theme of love. He tells us that every circumstance, every person, every opportunity has its special face of love. Those who know themselves to be inseparable from Blessed Energy will recognize this special quality because love calls to love. In the most painful circumstances, that love cries out and we respond with deliberate choice to the highest expression of unconditional love.

—Most Reverend Dr. Marilyn L. Sieg,
    Bishop, Old Catholic Church

"Many in your world have asked, 'What is channeling?' And many have been afraid of it and have said, 'Channeling is opening to things that I do not understand.' And that statement is very true in the world: the ego sees much to fear because it does not understand, cannot comprehend the Whole Self. Channeling is opening to a greater awareness of Who you are. In the Dream of the holy Child — which is Who you are — you drew an imaginary boundary, a boundary around the body and around the personality that you feel yourself to be, and have said, "This is all there is to me. This is who I am" — forgetting that you were the one who drew the boundary in the first place. You are the one defining the boundary. And in doing that, you have drawn a boundary in a great sea of beingness, the great sea of beingness which you are. That boundary exists nowhere except in your own mind and belief.

"When you open yourself to a greater awareness, you are opening yourself to the rest of the sea of Light and

Beingness. You go beyond the boundary for a moment or two when you sit in meditation and you feel an expanded sense of Self. You are going beyond the self-imposed boundary which you have put there, and you are tapping into the greater part of yourSelf. There is nothing outside of you. There is nothing outside of you. There is nothing to fear. Everything that you experience is in your consciousness and it is you."

...Chapter 1 "Channeling"

150 Pages, Paperback.... $12.95
ISBN 1-878555-08-1

Jeshua: The Personal Christ
Volume II

This enlightening book contains channeled information from Jeshua ben Joseph. Jesus talks about meditation, the descent into matter, falling in love, ascending in Love, the days to come, manifesting, the Age of Enlightenment, ascension, prayer and much more. **Foreword by Alan Cohen.**

There is nothing a human can do on this planet that is more spectacular than to examine the piece of god that resides in themselves. The loving Jeshua material is uplifting and powerful. This really is necessary reading in this new age!

— Lee Carroll - Channel for Kryon

"Beloved and holy Child of our Father, when first you thought to be upon what you now call our holy Mother, the Earth, you came as the Light being that you are. You came with the creativity of the holy Child to see, 'What more can I create?'

"For, verily, before time began, you, as the Child of the Creator, flexed your figurative creative wings, and as one great Thought to experience the beauty of energy in form, you imagined, put the images into action, and brought forth energy into form.

"Now, the Thought energy did not coalesce right away, for there would be — although this was just the beginning of what you have called time — eons of time before the form would come into what you now recognize and know. The Earth, the planets, the universes were/are very much a Light energy and you were/are Light energy, and the forms that you brought forth were nebulous, cloud-like. You knew yourself to be Light, and the creations were Light. You were very much one with what you are creating — for truly, it is not an event that has happened a long time ago; it is what is happening moment by moment as the Light and the Consciousness that you are.

"And as the Earth came into being, you thought to create upon and out of the substance of Earth. You thought to bring together frequencies and vibrations of the Light into various combinations to see what would result. And with those thoughts were born the clouds, the energies of the oceans, of the rivers, of the streams, and the more dense material known as the mountains and the hills in their various formations.

"In due time, you thought to experience life upon this plane, and you came as the Light being that you are. Not with the attraction of the molecules of physicality that you see yourself now surrounded by... but you came as the Light being to experience, "What would it feel like to be upon what I have created?" ...

... Chapter 4 "You've Gone As Far As You Can Go"

208 Pages, Paperback....$12.95
ISBN 1-878555-09-X

Jeshua: The Personal Christ
Volume III
Don't Look For Me In a Tortilla Chip

In this volume, Jeshua/Jesus explains the Bible in terms we can understand today. Passages such as the Ten Commandments, the Sermon on the Mount and the Beatitudes, Isaiah 40 (Comfort Ye My People) take on new and expanded meaning, and in a very personal way Jeshua/Jesus describes choosing His disciples, His baptism, His temptations and beginning His ministry. Everyone who wants to know Him better and to understand the writings of the Scriptures more fully will want to have this volume at their desk and bedside table.

Includes a special cameo chapter: Mother Mary talks about Holy Communion.

This is the time that the Christ Consciousness is revealing itself in many ways, blessing us with the wisdom we need to step into our own mastery and enlightenment. Judith Coates has listened to the 'still quiet voice' within, and in doing so has opened for us all the grace that lies within us all.

— James F. Twyman

"Child of our Father, there was a time in which I spoke unto you what has come to be known as The Sermon on the Mount. The Mount was a high place, a hill upon which we gathered so that the multitudes could be seated all around, for by this time many knew of the healings which had taken place and were anxious to learn of what I would teach.

"First, a word about the Scriptures which you have now. Know you that what you have recorded in your Holy Bible as to my teachings are someone's notes of what they remembered me saying. The words which you have extant in your Scriptures today, the words ascribed to me, are a compilation of remembrances, cryptic messages often preserved by oral tradition, handed down from one person to another. These messages were originally based on someone's summation of what they heard me teach, similar to the notes you have taken at some of your workshops and lectures.

"Further, know you that as your Scriptures have been handed down to you, seemingly by others and yet it has been an evolution in which you have participated, the translations which have been made and the words which have been chosen have often taken on different meanings than that which was originally intended. For example:

"Blessed are the poor in spirit.... Now, I did not say 'poor' in spirit. The word which I used meant simple, uncomplicated, un-complex. Blessed are the simple in spirit. For theirs is the Kingdom of Heaven, as they abide in the realm of uncomplicatedness...." –Chapter 2, "The Beatitudes"

82 Pages, Paperback....$12.95
ISBN 1-878555-12-X

Jeshua, The Personal Christ, Volume IV
The Interdimensional Self: The Way to Peace

In this monumental volume, Jesus talks about the interdimensional Self, the Beholder Self, which views all things from the perspective of Wholeness. The interdimensional Self is not attached to things, events, circumstances and individuals, but sees everything from a place of peace. Jeshua talks about the out-of-body experience, realities and the nature of Reality, living in the Mind of God, the healing consciousness (with a healing meditation), the True religion, Sacred Union, My Peace I Give Unto You, and Come unto Me, among other topics.

This work moves the reader in gentle steps toward a willingness to embrace an expanded understanding of Self. What else could be more important? What else are we yearning for? Some of these steps, such as mindfulness, are common knowledge. Some, such as the instruction to "play" and to let our imaginations and even our desire guide us, are less common.

With our acceptance of our belovedness we can extend this belovedness to one another and begin to move into the time that has not yet been written, the time of a new consciousness.

—Mari Perron, author of *The Course of Love* series

"In your process of awakening, which is happening now, it is time and it is imperative that you practice expanding the consciousness beyond just the individuality you have seen yourself to be. You are the one who has agreed to be the bridge person; you are the one who is remembering now that you have agreed to be the light even in the darkness of forgetfulness which is yet upon this plane, this reality. In your agreement, you have said that there will be a time when you will expand the consciousness beyond the individuality. That time is now. That is why you feel such a driving motivation within yourself to read, to study, to discuss, to contemplate, to seek, to want to know more. You have said, 'In the process of awakening, there will come a time when I will know that I am much more than the body, much more than the personality I have seen myself to be, much more than the personality I keep working on to make better, much more than the individuality that I know is most wonderful and yet I can't quite always be happy with it. There will come a time' — and this is now — 'when I will begin to expand my consciousness to know the interdimensionality, the Reality of me. I will come to know and to touch that space, the matrix, the Isness of me, the extension of the Father.'

"When you come to the full realization that the matrix of you, the interdimensionality of You which is not focused upon a dimension or a reality, when you come to the realization that, "I and the Father are One; I am an extension of the Father," when you come to realize that the matrix out of which you function and fashion everything which you experience is of the Isness of the Father, you become transformed."

...Chapter 2 Moving Into Interdimensional Consciousness

214 Pages, Paperback....$12.95
ISBN 1-878555-14-6

Jeshua, The Personal Christ, Volume V
You Are The Power Of The Future

In this intriguing volume, Jeshua speaks about the new Essenes, stages of empowerment, the Council of One, how to have a personal relationship with God, the dimensions of consciousness, the new consciousness, how you are the power of the future, and much more. **Includes an Interview with Judith Coates.**

Channeled wisdom, including the loving wisdom of our beloved Jeshua, asks us to acknowledge the confusion that exists in the world while filling our heart with the knowingness that we already are the change we wish to see. It is inherent within us. Bathed in this faith, we are made whole rather than responsible, trustworthy instead of doubt-filled. Those of us who have been touched and inspired by profound channeling have much to be grateful for. Hopeful and secure, it falls upon us to be the example for others that Jeshua is for us.

Pepper Lewis, Author, Visionary, Humanitarian.

Channel for Gaia's wisdom and teachings

"Collective consciousness has had certain belief about the future. It has always been thus, that collective consciousness has feared the future. But no longer do you have to fear the future. **You are the power of the future.** You have the power to make it as you want it to be. You are free to do that because you have come forth from the one creative Principle that creates all things.

"From this moment on you are free to change anything and all things. See your future as you want it to be. If a small bit of fear comes up, take your eraser of peace and erase it, and in its place put that which you want your future to hold.

You do not have to fear loss, abandonment, judgment. Those are of the world. Those are fears long acted out and completed. Those fears are done. You have lived them many lifetimes. So if the fear comes up about the future, erase it, and in its place put that which you desire. Surround it with love and know that you have the power to change it, because you have had the power to create your life – this life and all other lifetimes up to this point – as you desire and believe it to be."

--Chapter 24, "You are the Power of the Future"

208 Pages, Paperback $14.95
ISBN 978-878555-15-1

Jesus and Mastership
The Gospel According to Jesus of Nazareth

Jesus tells His story in His own words. Dictated through the Rev. James C. Morgan, Unity minister, this is the day to day account of Jesus' life from age 18, when He went to India to study, through the crucifixion and resurrection. He tells of choosing His disciples, His relationship with Miriam, His ministry and why He taught what He did. Now in its third printing. A best-seller, internationally. A new Bible.

A Message from Jesus of Nazareth to You, the Reader:

"I feel the account of my life on the earth plane about 2,000 years ago, given in this manner, will have more meaning and be more accurate than the messages I have inspired others to write. They were excellent channels, but this is a better way. Naturally, the language we are using is the current idiom rather than a translation of the Aramaic I spoke long ago. There will be no conjecture or supposing. It must be perfectly clear to anyone who reads this book that my sole purpose in living and giving of myself was to awaken man to his true potential.

"The people of that time were living in a state of mind that was quite similar to the state of mind of most people today. There were the rich and the poor, the well and the sick, those who worshipped many gods, those who worshipped one God, and those who worshipped none or self. Men were the rulers and women their chattel. There were the cruel and the gentle. There were those who hated and those who loved. Crime was rampant, and seemingly might ruled. Yes, it was much the same as today— there was happiness and there was sadness. There was much that was good and there was that which was not so good. At that, it was a good world for mankind in which to learn and grow.

"This is only a very meager description of the kind of world into which I incarnated. I returned to the earth plane with an intense desire to help man raise himself to a better life and to realize his own vast and unlimited spiritual powers. These powers were being used incorrectly and thus bringing undesirable conditions forth into the lives of a large portion of mankind.

"I believed that I should stir the people up to awaken them to their own spiritual self just as I had found mine. So this is the reason I took the action that I did. I knew it would create commotion and call attention to what I was teaching.

"Mankind must know the truth and not someone's interpretation of what I said or meant. It is time for all men to make ready for the new age coming by the year 2,000. Only those who accept the living God as their creator and saviour will survive the worldwide tribulations that are coming. Those who grow spiritually will reach the heights of glory in God's kingdom of peace and happiness. All others will be in turmoil and pain of their own choosing...."

...Introductory Message

352 Pages, Paperback....$14.95
ISBN 1-878555-00-6

Return Passage
Journey of the Soul
By Michael Harvey

An engrossing novel of reincarnation: lifetimes of power, passion and intrigue, in Atlantis, in Galilee, etc., culminating with a modern day incarnation which illumines all lifetimes. The final chapter will surprise you with a beautiful twist of an ending.

Have you ever tried to explain reincarnation to someone? This book does it easily.

This book is beautifully written, very empowering and inspirational. After reading it, you will have no choice but to deeply honor the path you are on and love yourself and everyone in your life a little more. Highly recommended!

— Bookstore, Seattle, Washington

"The first report came from Mu. A huge earthquake of 9.6 magnitude had devastated islands to the north. The casualties were enormous. Air and sea rescue units were being mobilized to assist survivors. Mu itself was bracing for a gigantic tidal wave. We looked in horror as the extent of the damage became apparent. The few survivors interviewed told of horrendous loss of life and property.

"The following morning newscasts centered on rescue attempts and the magnitude of damage. So far, the expected tidal wave hadn't materialized. The first newscast received in space was a rehash of news I'd seen earlier. I was ready to turn off the set when the program was interrupted by an important news flash. Another devastating quake had ripped the southern Pole. Again the quake was of unprecedented magnitude. It was so strong the recorder was unable to measure the intensity. If this were indeed true and not a malfunction of the recording equipment, nothing could have withstood the quake.

"Still glued to the television monitor, my mind drifted to my stupidity a couple of days ago. What had possessed me to succumb to such irrational emotions? Sinta had asked to speak to me with such urgency I couldn't refuse her. Normally drones only reply when spoken to, but again she displayed the animation I'd witnessed when she'd related her faith in a Creator.

"I led her out of earshot of the household as a citizen didn't talk to a drone unless it was to give instructions. Again I noticed the astounding fact of an intensity and intelligence shining in the blueness of her eyes.

'Please,' she implored, 'take me to Master Noah. The time has arrived.' What was she talking about, what lunacy was Noah involved in? How on earth had he contacted her? "What are you talking about, Sinta?" She took my hand in hers (again an action no drone was permitted) and without hesitation explained her request.

'Noah,' she said, 'is calling all true believers. I can hear him distinctly in my head. All The Ones now have this ability.' Flabbergasted, I demanded to know if she now considered herself a member of The Ones, who, to my knowledge were all human and certainly not drones. 'Oh, yes,' she replied...."

...Chapter 15

232 Pages, Paperback....$12.95
ISBN 1-878555-02-2

Books from Oakbridge University Press can be ordered directly online at: www.oakbridge.org or by calling 253-952-3285.

**Yes, I would like to order the following books:
Please send (quantity)**

____ **Jeshua: The Personal Christ I** $12.95

____ **Jeshua: The Personal Christ II** $12.95

____ **Jeshua: The Personal Christ III** $12.95

____ **Jeshua: The Personal Christ IV** $12.95

____ **Jeshua: The Personal Christ V** $14.95

____ **Jesus and Mastership** $14.95

____ **Return Passage** $12.95

Please include postage of $2.50 media rate or $5.00 for priority mailing.

Enclosed is $_____

Name _____

Address _____

City _____ State _____ Zip____

Telephone _____

Visa/MasterCard/Discover Card information:

Account #_____

Expiration ____/_____

Signature _____